THE CREDIBILIT

How to understand the men in your business life —
and win with your own rules

THE *CREDIBILITY* *GAP*

How to Understand the Men
in Your Business Life
—and Win with Your Own Rules

KATHRYN B. STECHERT

THORSONS PUBLISHING GROUP
Wellingborough, Northamptonshire

Rochester, Vermont

First published 1986 as *Sweet Success* by Macmillan Publishing Company, 866 Third Avenue, New York, N.Y. 10022

This edition first published in Great Britain 1987

British Library Cataloguing in Publication Data

Stechert, Kathryn
[Sweet success]. The credibility gap: how
to understand the men in your business
life — and win with your own rules.
1. Success in business   2. Women in business
I. [Sweet success]   II. Title
650.1'024042   HF5386

ISBN 0-7225-1506-5

Printed and bound in Great Britain

This book is dedicated to Maurine Royce
and in memory of Hayes Royce.

CONTENTS

PREFACE

One February a few years ago I was lazing on a beach in Puerto Rico, making conversation with a fellow vacationer on the adjoining chaise longue. As the woman and I talked, our attention was drawn to two boys, about six or seven years old, playing with unrestrained high spirits at the water's edge. The boys chased each other back and forth on the beach, falling, tussling, and throwing fistfuls of sand at one another. One of them, in his exuberance, picked up a handful of sand and tossed it in his *own* face, laughing and screaming. The woman said, to herself as much as to me, "My daughter would never play like that. Until I had a child of my own I never would have said that boys and girls are fundamentally different—but I know it now. My daughter just wouldn't be so rambunctious."

The incident was, in a way, the beginning of this book. After years of hearing women talk of nonsexist childrearing, that mother's comment was a surprise. I began to think about how the sexes are different in significant ways that affect behavior. And when I began to mention it to other women, I found they were noticing what I had been noticing—and, more significant, were ready to talk about it.

In the course of research for articles I had written about women and work, I had begun to see that many of the problems of working women involved their relationships with men on the job. And I suspected those problems had something to do with sex differences. In their personal lives women constantly make an effort to understand men, and, more important, they rarely, if ever, assume that men will behave as women would in the same situations. Although that thinking hasn't extended to the workplace yet, it seems to me that it's time it did. We have grown so accustomed to insisting that women can do and be anything a man can that we have been blind to differences that affect our work relationships with men. Worse, we have failed to examine the differences and to use them to our benefit.

Indeed, women are capable of performing any job a man can, and women must continue to resist those who use sex differences as an excuse for keeping women out of high-paying and high-status jobs. The manual dexterity of women that makes them good typists should also make them good brain surgeons. The "people skills" that make women good teachers should also make them good managers. What keeps women out of the higher ranks in business and the professions, however, is not an inability to perform certain tasks, or even a lack of education and experience, but rather a complex knot of discrimination, expectation, and, I suggest, a failure to understand men and how they work. Most positions of power are still filled by men, and if women are to succeed they must understand how men operate. This book is about what women must know about men to relate to them comfortably and effectively. It is also about how sex differences influence those relationships.

As part of my research I interviewed working women in a variety of jobs in different parts of the country. One of the questions I asked was whether they thought men were different from them in ways that affected work. Many women were hesitant to talk at first—it seemed a trick question—and many prefaced their comments with a disclaimer of some sort, such as, "I'm sure it's just my boss, but here's what he does . . ." or "I doubt most men are like this, but the guys in my office . . ." But following that, what the women I talked to said was, yes, the men they worked with were different and it was those differences that often confused women and caused problems between the sexes. Each woman considered her experiences to be unique, and of course they are. But I began to see remarkable similarities among the experiences of women in widely different kinds of jobs. A woman who was vice president in a company employing hundreds of people told me stories the same as those I heard from a woman worker in a seven-person office.

One woman spoke with passion for two hours about the frustrations she encountered at work because her male bosses and colleagues seemed to have fundamentally different values and seemed unable to relate to her in ways that made her comfortable and happy in her job. The woman must have felt she had revealed more than she wanted to, because a few days after our conversation I received a letter from her and a copy of an essay by a prominent feminist calling for androgyny and the coming together of the sexes. In her letter the woman said that instead of dwelling on the differences between men and women, the sexes would be better off if they could "merge," a goal she saw as a "broader, more forgiving and loving vision." That is a powerful sentiment, but one at odds with the experiences of both women and men. Perhaps we could live without conflict if we were all alike—if there were no racial or religious or cultural differences. But those differences exist—and they are valuable. We are not all alike, and differences between the sexes may be among the most significant between people.

To conduct research for this book I also turned to the work of psychologists, anthropologists, social scientists, linguists, and other scholars. I found a surprising amount of study being done on sex differences. This book relates that research to the workplace and backs up those findings with experiences from the daily lives of working women. Finally, it offers suggestions on how women can use what they've learned about male behavior and sex differences to get along with—and get what they want from—men.

Ideally, women and men will one day come to respect and value the differences between them. Until then, I hope this book helps working women correct the imbalance in the workplace that so often puts men ahead of them. Above all, I hope the future will see women getting more of what they need and deserve at work: power, money, respect, credibility, satisfaction, and pleasure.

Kathryn Stechert

ACKNOWLEDGMENTS

The voices and experiences of dozens of women appear in this book; some are named and so their contributions are obvious. But most are not. For various reasons they, as well as a number of men I interviewed, requested anonymity. I am indebted to all who granted me interviews, sometimes quite lengthy, and who shared valuable and significant information.

The foundation of this book rests on the work of many scholars in the fields of social science, psychology, linguistics, and anthropology. Although I am grateful to them all, I especially want to acknowledge the work of Carol Gilligan, whose book *In a Different Voice* greatly influenced my thinking.

I wish to thank Krystyna Poray Goddu, Susan Renner-Smith, and Marian Faux, who read early drafts of the manuscript, for their ideas, many editorial contributions, and for their friendship. Suzanne Burger provided significant help with my search of the scientific literature on sex differences and with other research; I could not have met my deadlines without her.

Dominick Abel, my literary agent, was indispensable from the very beginning, when this book was just an idea. I am also grateful to my editors at Macmillan, Arlene Friedman and Melinda Corey, for their guidance.

Finally, special thanks to Robert Stechert, for his insights, encouragement, and unfailing good humor.

PART ONE
UNDERSTANDING MEN

1 HOW MEN AND WOMEN DIFFER

When Linda* started her job as an announcer at a radio station, she entered an all-male world for the first time. One of her immediate observations was that the men never offered support or encouragement to one another or to her. No one even said anything as simple as, "You look tired today," much less, "You did a great job," which was what she most wanted to hear.

Linda also noticed that the atmosphere at the station was often tense; she thought at least part of the reason must have been because no one talked about their feelings or praised others. "All we would hear," she says, "were the complaints from the businessmen about how the station handled their commercials."

So Linda made an effort to give her co-workers the treatment she wished for herself. She frequently complimented one colleague who was her favorite on-air person. After a few compliments, though, he began to stiffen whenever she approached him after his show and told him how much she liked his work. She assumed he was shy and didn't know how to handle the admiration, but she figured that he was secretly pleased and strengthened by the support, just as she would have been. Some weeks later he finally took her aside and asked her to stop; he said he didn't need her esteem. What she had intended as caring attention appeared to him to be fulsome praise. What was wrong with his work if suddenly it needed so much boosting?

The effect of Linda's behavior, though well motivated, was to

---

*First name pseudonyms used to protect the identities of those requesting anonymity.

make the men she worked with uneasy. She had failed to understand one simple, essential fact about men: They are different from women.

Sex differences in behavior, language, value systems, and psychology greatly affect the conduct of men and women at work. Not understanding men gets working women into trouble again and again. Had Linda realized that the men she worked with did not necessarily have the same needs and ways of expressing themselves that she did, she could more easily have dealt with the frustration of getting no feedback about her work. She also would have spared the men considerable discomfort and, perhaps, advanced her career more quickly.

Understanding how men differ from women—in the ways they think, feel, express themselves, view the world, and, thus, do business—may be a woman's most important key to career success. If she understands the motivations and behavior of men and can interpret the signals they give out about what they're thinking and feeling, she can use that knowledge to her advantage in reaching her career goals.

EQUAL, BUT DIFFERENT

Linda didn't know what she was doing wrong with her male colleagues because she assumed they were like her. That's not surprising: Like many women, she tries to minimize differences between the sexes rather than to examine and understand them. Men and women have much to learn about one another and how to work together. Men, of course, have at least as much to learn about women as women do about men, but men don't have the same motivation to learn. Because men dominate the workplace, the status quo suits them well. They got there first and set the patterns and rules according to what pleases them. It's up to women to take the initiative in learning to understand men's ways.

Learning them will be easier if we can let go an assumption that no longer serves us well, that is, any differences between women and men, other than the obvious physical ones needed for reproduction, are insignificant and to be ignored. This assumption grew from the efforts of feminists in the sixties who stressed the similarities between the sexes. At that time, the critical need was to convince men—and women—that women were as capable as men and should have equal opportunity to strive for good jobs and responsible roles. The best way to do that was to insist that women were no different from men. As a consequence, the struggle to promote equality resulted in the conclusion that equality couldn't exist without sameness. To be different was to be unequal. And for women to be different from men at work was to be wrong.

Circumstances have changed and that old idea is giving way to one that provides for greater recognition and understanding of gender differences. Over the past twenty years women have done a good job of telling men what they were doing that offended and harmed women. We told them that sexual harassment in all its forms was demeaning and damaging to women. We told them that assuming women should serve men was inappropriate at work. We told them they weren't hiring women in numbers that reflected their skills and education. We told them women expected and deserved to be paid what men were paid. And those messages penetrated. Although women's problems on the job are far from being solved, at least today there are fewer distinctions in sex roles than there were twenty years ago—women drive trucks, men rear children.

That doesn't, however, diminish the many underlying sex differences. Although men and women may be freer to take on various roles, they won't necessarily perform them the same way. Recognizing that women may do a job as well as, but differently from, men, and that men's ways aren't the only methods, is essential if women are to achieve more, if they are to continue to advance in their careers, and if they are to open that last tier of doors that has remained closed to them. Today women want not only the jobs, but the promotions. They want access not just to low- and middle-management positions, but to senior management as well. Taking that next step, however, requires that we recognize rather than deny sex differences.

During the sixties and seventies, when women began to enter the work force in large numbers and with high ambition, many women assumed that to be successful they had to imitate men. And many began by dressing in pin-striped suits and foulard ties, memorizing sports and military jargon, participating in assertiveness seminars, and affecting a tough, no-nonsense manner. To be an imitation or substitute man, however, is to be doomed to be second best. Even the most ordinary male makes a better man than a woman does. And the reverse, fortunately, is also true. But the man's way is not the only way, even—perhaps especially—in business. As one high-level female executive says, "I think we can bring something more to the party."

As women gain strength, confidence, and experience in business, they are coming to recognize and acknowledge sex differences. "A lot of people say there's no difference between men and women in the workplace," says Carolyn Carter, vice president and management supervisor at Grey Advertising in New York. "They say there are just differences between good and bad. But that's a lot of hogwash."

Discoveries about how the sexes differ are not returning us to pre-liberation days when "men were men and women were glad of it," but instead are opening up a new era where the extent and significance of gender differences can be acknowledged and studied and, most important, where the information can be used by all of us to work together in greater accord and effectiveness. A woman doesn't need to be *like* a man to succeed; she needs to understand men and to be herself.

The sexes differ in numerous large and small ways. Before examining some of the specific topics that will help women at work, such as how the sexes differ in their uses of humor and language, and how they differ in psychological development, it is useful to take a look at what scientists have discovered recently about how the sexes differ. These findings all confirm one point: Science is on its way toward documenting what, philosophical vagaries aside, has been observed to be true throughout the ages—females and males do, from time to time, behave differently in significant ways.

THE AGGRESSIVE SEX

In an extensive survey, published in 1974, of research on sex differences, psychologists Eleanor Emmons Maccoby and Carol Nagy Jacklin concluded that there are four well-established differences between the sexes: Girls have greater verbal ability; boys excel in visual/spatial ability; boys excel in mathematical ability; and, in study after study, males are shown to be more aggressive than females. All those differences could affect men and women at work. The most significant factor, however, may be men's greater aggressiveness, because of the wide-reaching effect of aggression on behavior.

Both physically and verbally, males show themselves to be the aggressive sex. Boys demonstrate more attenuated forms of aggression, like mock fighting and aggressive fantasies, as well as direct forms. The difference is found as early as age two, when social play begins.

Maccoby and Jacklin define aggression as a variety of actions and motives that have a theme of intent to hurt another. The attempts to hurt can be based on a desire to hurt for its own sake or a desire to control the other person. Hostility can be expressed in many ways— from vindictive daydreams to physical attack to overt but highly disguised expressions, such as hostile words and malicious actions.

Years of research, since the 1930s, in a variety of cultures have turned up consistent evidence that males are more aggressive than females. One cross-cultural study of behavior reported in 1974, for example, showed that in all cultures studied, physical assault of one child upon another was rare, but boys engaged in more mock fighting, rough-and-tumble play, and more verbal insults, and were more likely than girls to counterattack if someone else behaved aggressively toward them either verbally or physically.

A comparison of crime and death statistics suggests greater violence in men's lives, too. More than four times as many men as women die of homicide in this country. And although the number of women arrested for white-collar crimes, such as fraud and embezzlement, is rising rapidly, men still account for nearly nine out of ten arrests for violent crimes. For example, for every 2 women arrested for murder, there are 12 men arrested; for every 28 women arrested for aggravated assault, 186 men are arrested. Whether women lack the inclination—or merely the opportunity—for violence cannot necessarily be determined from such statistics, although they do point to greater aggression in males.

OTHER DIFFERENCES

The sexes differ in many other ways that may or may not affect how they work together. Women, for instance, outlive men, always have, and it seems always will, since the gap between female and male longevity is widening, rather than narrowing. A male born in 1950 was expected to live 65.5 years and a female 71 years; those figures compare with 70 and 78 years for 1983 babies.

Odd, apparently unconnected, and often unexplained reports turn up in scientific journals that point to highly specific sex differences. Females, for example, seem to have more tactile sensitivity. They have better finger dexterity as well. And women cry more often than men, four times more, according to one researcher. Many experiments show women to be more practiced in using verbal skills to deal with emotions; women also seem to act upon their emotions with more consistency, whereas males are more likely to discount feelings. Perhaps because women seem to feel emotions with more intensity and to respond to others with more empathy, they are also stressed more by their own emotions and feel the emotions of others more, including the painful ones. More and more, gender is recognized as a significant variable in any study of humans.

WHERE DO SEX DIFFERENCES COME FROM?

Scientists are not only struggling to find out *how* the sexes differ, they are trying to find out *why*. And while there is much agreement that gender differences do exist in sexual orientation, behavior, and cognitive function, there is little agreement on the source of those differences. Explanations for typical male behavior range from the effects of testosterone on the brain to womb envy to fathers who fear homosexuality and won't let their boys play with dolls.

Cross-cultural studies that show males are more aggressive than females seem a strong argument for saying male aggression is rooted in biology, and yet one recent ongoing study is failing to turn up a correlation between the level of sex hormones and the amount of aggression in boys, as earlier studies have.

Some researchers don't try to account for the differences. One psychologist, for example, whose research showed that females seem to be better at articulating emotions than men, doesn't attempt to explain it. He says the cause could be physical differences in male and female brains. On the other hand, he suggests, the differences may exist because boys are discouraged from talking about emotions. They simply may not learn how to make the connections between emotions and words the way girls do.

We will probably never know precisely what accounts for sex differences. Evidence that they are due to both nature *and* nurture is strong. What makes us men and women may have a lot to do with sex hormones, but also with how we grow up. And the childhood experiences of males and females are very different. We grow up in different environments and with different sensibilities and activities. While the boys were roughhousing and comparing the strengths of their throwing arms, we were at slumber parties imagining, conversing, and sharing secrets. While we were endlessly dressing and undressing our dolls and inventing elaborate lives and activities for them, the boys were racing bicycles and pushing rocks down hills for the pleasure of watching them fall. Because no one will ever raise a child without culture in the ultimate experiment to determine the effects of nature and nurture, we'll never have the full answers. Even the anthropologist Melvin Konner, who has studied and understands the force of biology on gender as well as anyone, writes, "If I ask myself why I feel like a man, the answer has something to do with testosterone but something also to do with the way Cary Grant and Katharine Hepburn behaved in the films I grew up on."

What matters for today's working woman is that she recognize sex differences and learn to take them into account. Even if the forces that shape males and females are merely the result of social conditioning and sexual stereotypes that years of nonsexist childrearing will eradicate, the fact is that the differences exist today, and they affect women's daily work lives.

NO SEX DIFFERENCES, TOO

The sexes differ in some significant and intriguing ways that affect them in their jobs and daily lives, but when talking about sex differences, we must remember that the distinctions are generalities. Overall trends don't necessarily hold for individuals. *Every* man is not more aggressive than *every* woman; nor is every woman more verbally skilled than every man. It's also important to remember that the sexes do not differ in certain significant ways.

In *The Psychology of Sex Differences*, Maccoby and Jacklin deflate cliché after cliché regarding how men and women differ. Both feminists, they set out to dispel myths about differences in the popular view and succeeded in deflating the crippling belief that women were not as capable as men. No studies show that either sex has superior intellectual capacity. Both males and females direct their achievement efforts toward similar goals, and both work to the same extent because of interest in the task rather than for approval. Although there is slight evidence that females have better memory when a task involves verbal content, it cannot be said that either sex has a better memory overall or a better system for storage and retrieval of information.

Because the sexes do *not* differ in significant ways, it might seem on the surface that we would be better off stressing the similarities and de-emphasizing the differences. After all, the more alike groups of people are, the easier it seems to be for them to get along. And certainly what women have sought for decades is to be treated with the same regard as men and given the same opportunities. When we admit to differences we open up the opportunity for comparison. If any two things are different, the question "Which is *better*?" seems to follow even without our willing it. What women and men must do, however, is resist that impulse to judge and learn to accept and respect sex differences.

Differences need not be feared, nor should they be used to demonstrate the inferiority of either sex. Typical female qualities of caring, nurturance, and lack of aggression are to be valued—in the workplace and in personal relationships. To deny them is to discount some of the best and essential qualities of humanity. It is far better for both sexes to embrace the differences and use them to their fullest. If we don't learn to acknowledge sex differences, women will forever be judged by a male standard and will forever come up lacking. And nowhere will that be more damaging than at work.

BARRIERS IN THE WORKPLACE

Although women have moved into the work force in huge numbers and made significant gains in winning rights, breaking down barriers, and gaining access to jobs, few women have moved into positions of power and influence. Women-owned businesses account for just 3 percent of the nation's economy. At the current rate that women are elected to Congress, more than four hundred years will pass before half of Congress is female. And only one *Fortune* 500 company is headed by a woman. Even in traditional fields women are not faring particularly well. Eighty-three percent of elementary school teachers are still women and 81 percent of school principals are men.

In the more than twenty years since the Equal Pay Act was initiated, women have made little progress in closing the wide wage gap. The average full-time working woman earns 62 cents for each dollar earned by the average man. That's just pennies higher than when the law was passed in 1963. In a study of 91 occupations, selected because there were enough men and women employed in each to compare earnings, not *one* showed women's median income equal to or more than men's. An analysis of census data, released in January 1984, indicates that there was actually more wage discrimination against young white women who entered the labor force in 1980 than in 1970. Black women, who are even further behind white women, made slight progress.

Women have moved into entry-level jobs in fields throughout the country, but management continues to be a new frontier—and sometimes a bleak one. The cover of the April 16, 1984 issue of *Fortune* magazine depicted the plight of women striving for high-level positions. The image: a dressed-for-success woman on a ladder reaching for a broken rung.

A 1982 *Business Week*/Harris poll of 602 high-ranking corporate officials presented a more optimistic, though not more realistic, picture. The poll showed, according to the magazine, that "top executives affirm that despite a decade of doubts that women could perform well as managers, they have, in fact, succeeded." The survey respondents, all from the 1,200 largest companies in the country, agreed overwhelmingly with the statements: "Contributions of women executives in the company are more positive than negative"; and, "Women executives are performing on the job as well as or better than expected." Such findings led the magazine to exult: "Business votes 'yes' on women as executives."

Pollster Louis Harris warned, however, that the results needed to be interpreted with caution, because the executives surveyed were so high in the corporations (about two-thirds were CEOs) that they were not professionally threatened by competition from women executives.

Analyzing the data, Harris found two kinds of questions. One type probed for official corporate policy on hiring women executives; those received overwhelmingly positive answers. Harris says that executives voice "the litany, the conventional rhetoric" expertly and sincerely.

The other type of question, which asked about practices that reflect how things are really done, revealed a deep split. Harris says, "The division is really between hiring and promoting." For example, 41 percent agreed with this statement: "It has been harder to promote women to high-level positions than we thought it would be." When the data were broken down into various areas, it showed that in traditional male industries, like manufacturing, a majority of executives said promoting women had been harder than they expected. And still the *Business Week* reporter persisted in seeing the survey as good news for women, saying the survey results were far different from what might have been expected ten or even five years ago. The magazine concluded: "At the level of the largest U.S. companies, at least, top executives are making a determined effort to focus on performance rather than on perceived differences between men and women executives."

Nevertheless, even women who never doubted their ability to measure up to men in performance are finding that mere competence is not enough. One thirty-year-old woman, who in just six years reached upper management in a large company, says, "All the barriers I thought wouldn't be there by the time *I* made it *are* there." She found that the most difficult barriers are the intangibles, the attitudes of men. Such women are frustrated and confused when they see themselves and women like them—strong, competent, committed to their work, well-educated, eager to move up, and willing to make the necessary sacrifices—still not moving ahead with the speed and sureness that would seem to go along with such dedication to purpose. What's holding them back? Lack of education in one all-important area: the ways in which men differ from women.

Women simply are not gaining power with the speed and in the numbers they could and should be. An imbalance remains in the work world. Part of the reason for that imbalance is that women have been plugging along, trying to act like men, assuming they should do business like men, and ignoring the different ways in which men and women work.

2 UNDERSTANDING MEN'S CONVERSATIONAL STYLES

Talking about her role in the film *Testament*, for which she was nominated for an Academy Award, Jane Alexander noted that it was the first time in 75 roles on screen and stage that she had been directed by a woman. The director/actor relationship was the easiest one she had ever experienced, partly because she could use a "shortcut in communication" with her director, Lynne Littman.

There may have been many reasons for that ease in communication, but one of them almost certainly was that Alexander and Littman were speaking the same language—which doesn't always happen with men and women. In fact, the sexes differ so greatly in the manner, and sometimes even in the substance, of their conversations that each sex can be said to have its own language.

The dissimilar experiences of women and men, their varying interests, and ways of relating to others, are revealed in their language. The differences are often in degrees of power, too. Men not only *are* more powerful in many circumstances, but they *expect* to be. And their language reflects that desire to dominate.

IT'S NOT EASY TO SAY WHAT YOU MEAN

Any conversation, no matter what the sex of the participants, poses certain risks and dangers. That's because everyone—in business as well as personal conversation—uses a technique linguists call "indirectness."

Indirectness is a way of speaking that falls between coming right out and baldly demanding or stating something, and sitting by, hoping

15

someone will read your mind. The technique is useful, because you can let someone know your desires without risking confrontation or rejection if the other person won't go along with you. Problems arise, though, when the indirectness is too subtle—or when the listener refuses to pick up the intended meaning. Indirectness can result in failure to communicate accurately; and its use can create problems in the workplace.

One woman, for example, wanted to take a long vacation in September, a time when she knew the work load in her office would be heavy. She explained to her boss that this particular trip was a one-time-only opportunity and she wanted very much to take it, even though she knew it was not the best timing.

He responded: "It really would make it tough on other people here. I don't think it's a very good idea, but why don't you think it over."

He wanted to say no, but didn't want to upset or confront her, so he used indirectness, hoping she'd get the message.

She didn't (either because he was too subtle or because she simply didn't want to hear "no"). A couple of days later she went to his office and said she had thought over her vacation request and she was sure she could keep control of her work. She did indeed intend to take her vacation in September.

His response was still not a simple "No, you may not." Instead, he replied coldly, "All right, but you're making a big mistake."

The woman got the message that time and changed her plans, but the mixed-up messages left her and her boss wary of one another.

In the instance cited, the woman's boss happened to be a man, but the same muddled communication could have occurred with another woman. Linguist Deborah Tannen says that indirectness makes all conversation "an activity comparable to picking your way through a minefield, but the minefield is particularly hazardous in talk between men and women." Although many people expect to stumble in communication with people from different countries and take extra care to be sure they understand and are understood, few realize that talk between men and women is cross-cultural, too. That's partly because the experiences of males and females are very different, for as Tannen puts it, "We grow up in different worlds, even if we grow up in the same house."

Boy Talk and Girl Talk

Women and men get twisted and tangled in their attempts at communication, because they use conversation for different purposes and because they often don't talk about the same subjects.

The primary difference between the way men and women use talk is this: Males like to talk about things and activity; females prefer to talk about people and feelings. Those distinctions show up at very early ages. Even in preschool, psychologists have found, boys are already talking about the physical environment and about activity. They talk about what they're building or the games they're playing. Little boys, who mostly play in groups, use their talk to set up rules for games and to discuss who's better at what. Their talk is auxiliary to activity.

For little girls, talk often is the activity. Girls tend to play in twos, using shared secrets to establish and maintain friendships. They talk about their own feelings and those of others; they talk about relationships between people (who likes whom, who's mad at whom, what the momma doll said to the little girl doll).

Those differences extend into adulthood and into the workplace. Describing the talk that men in her office use among themselves and that seems to make them comfortable, one woman says: "It's not getting-to-know-you kind of bantering. It's not intimate talk. It's surface talk, but it serves to build some type of camaraderie."

Women often establish business relationships through personal conversation. "Women assume you're interested in their personal lives," says one woman. "When you start a new job it's easy to find out right away about the other women. Men don't assume you're interested in their lives—and they aren't interested in yours."

A woman can get into trouble at work using the same techniques with a man that she would to establish a friendly relationship with a woman. Men often don't want to reveal the details of their lives and are put off by a co-worker who asks, "How are you feeling?" or, worse, "What's your problem?" Just the suggestion of chatting about emotions is likely to make a man uneasy. In the same way, a man is unlikely to want to hear about a woman's emotional life.

Women establish trust with one another through self-disclosure; they share secrets and problems and search for common feelings and experiences. Men, on the other hand, build trust through action. They want to know: Were you with me in the trenches? Will you support me in difficult situations? And they don't find that out through conversation as women do. Only time and experience will tell them what they really want to know about a person. Meanwhile, women who aren't savvy to the ways of men are busy trying to establish trust through disclosure—and men aren't willing to disclose anything until the trust is well established.

One man remembers being made uneasy by a female co-worker who didn't seem to know the nondisclosure code. One Monday morning he and a couple of male colleagues were standing around talking about the weekend. One offered that he had spent most of the time working in his yard; another said he had taken his son to a baseball game. The conversation was humming along until the woman colleague happened by and someone said, "Hey, Jean, how did your weekend go?" Her much-too-honest response was, "Not so great. Larry and I took our boat out to the lake yesterday and got in such a big fight that it ruined the day." The men hurried back to their offices before she could make the situation more awkward with additional detail. The man who tells this story points out that it was six months after the fact when he learned that the man in the office next to him had separated from his wife; and even then he got the news indirectly. His co-worker sent out Christmas cards carrying a new return address and signed with only one name—his.

It's not just personal lives and the emotions they entail that make men uncomfortable. They're just as likely to resist talking about the emotions that are a part of the job. Linda, a woman who worked almost exclusively with men as an announcer at a radio station, was continually frustrated by the refusal of her boss and male peers to talk about (and thus, in her mind, deal with) the emotions the work generated. "The emotional problems simply weren't talked about. It's a highly emotional job. You listen to music all day (and music is very emotional), people call in loving or hating what you're playing. Everyone at the station was high-pitched and there was no release for it. Emotions affected our business life and were a legitimate part of our business. I felt we had to talk about it, but the men wouldn't." Pushing them to talk about what bothered *her* only drove the men to be more closed.

Women can get into trouble in another way by talking about themselves and their emotions in business situations. A number of studies confirm that women do indeed disclose more personal information than men do; women tend to initiate more intimate questions and respond with more personal detail about themselves. Research also shows that women, after a self-disclosure conversation, feel a kinship with the conversation partner, but men feel less compatibility. Other studies indicate that subordinates are generally more self-revealing. Powerful people—women and men—keep their guard up. They don't use emotional displays or reveal personal information because such information gives others power over them.

There is one topic, however, about which men do permit themselves to lose their heads.

Man Talk

Ask any woman what the men in her office talk about when they're not talking about work and you're likely to hear "sports." Says one female vice president: "There's a lot of backslapping and talk like: 'Have you been fishing lately?' and 'Did you see the Cowboys play last night?' "

Ask a man what he talks about with co-workers and you'll get the same answer. One man said he and his colleagues talked about "any number of things''—and then described a conversation that involved any number of sports. "We talked about Carl Lewis at lunch one day and one guy didn't know who he was so the rest of us got all over him, because how could anyone not know who Carl Lewis was? We also talk about hockey and football. One guy went to Notre Dame and still goes to see them play a lot so we talk about that; if you went to Notre Dame you have to know a lot about sports. So there's lunchtime talk.''

Sports don't even have to be a big part of a man's life to be important to his conversation. One man, an executive who hasn't attended a sporting event in more than a year, who usually watches the World Series on television but often misses the season's opening game, and who rarely watches a football game on TV or elsewhere, says he often talks about sports with other men. "Sports is always a good icebreaker, a way to get things going," he says. "If I go to Washington and there's somebody in a senator's office I need to talk to but have never met I can always say, 'Hey, didn't the Caps do great in their game against the whosits last night?' Nine times out of ten the guy knows about the Caps and we can talk awhile. Whether you go to a barber or to meet a new client, sports is a safe topic of common interest. It's just natural; everybody's interested in sports.'' Just natural to most males, maybe, but not necessarily to many women who might not have the slightest notion what a man means when he says, "In the meeting, I want you to give a full-court press on this item.''

Sports Metaphors

Sports is more than just a handy icebreaker in conversation. It also forms the basis of many of the metaphors men use continually. Expressions such as, "Are you willing to go to the mat on this one?," "He's playing hardball," and "You're going to have to make some hard calls," are common to men's speech. Using sports metaphors in their conversations helps men remind one another that they have shared interests and experiences, but such figures of speech also are an efficient and economical use of language. If everyone understands a simile, it can be an effective way to convey an idea.

The problem for women, of course, comes when they don't understand. And they often don't, because they don't share the vocabulary. What should a woman do when men use expressions she doesn't understand? Dr. Jerie McArthur, who teaches management education seminars at the University of Minnesota, says that if a woman can get by without letting on that she doesn't know what was meant, she should. She can ask a trusted male friend later to explain the figure of speech. The risk, McArthur says, is that a woman doesn't know how dumb she may sound, how basic the metaphor is. She advises women, even those who don't have an interest in sports, to learn as much of the jargon as they can. Sports talk so pervades male business conversations that a woman who works with men is unlikely to be able to avoid it.

Even if a woman who has no interest in sports is careful about trying to remember the jargon, she may find herself, sooner or later, in a situation where she *must* know what the men are talking about and doesn't.

That happened to Carolyn Carter of Grey Advertising, who readily admits to being "a nonathlete." Carter was presenting a piece of advertising to a client and a group of people, mostly men, from her agency. The category manager for the client—a key person in the decision about whether the company would accept the advertising—looked at the story board presented and said: "This is the Dave Kingman board." Says Carolyn: "Little did I know that Dave Kingman was this baseball player who either hit a home run or struck out every time he got up to bat, which was how the client saw this piece of advertising. In the testing, it would either be fantastic, or it would be a zero."

The men continued to discuss the ad in terms of athletes, pulling in other names that were equally unfamiliar to Carter: "Yes, yes, Dave Kingman," one would say; or "No, it's more like [some other ball player]." None of this talk was giving her a clue to what they thought of the proposal.

"I let it go on for about three minutes," Carolyn says, "and then I said, *'Who is Dave Kingman?'* They looked at me with exaggerated pity, but they did explain it and the meeting went on from there."

Carter's response to this incident was not to take a crash course in baseball or to try following the sports pages (she still doesn't know what team Kingman plays for). Talking with the guys about sports just doesn't fit her style. "You can't try to be a man," she says. "I don't take my clients to football games. I take them to the theater. If I try to be a man, I'm sure to lose—so why do it? I have to be myself."

A woman who doesn't have an interest in sports is better off not trying to fake one, but a woman who does know something about the subject can use that to her advantage. One business owner who grew up with brothers in an athletic family says, "I don't find it a chore to check the sports pages in the morning. And if I'm going to lunch with a man who I know is interested in sports I'll check. If he's a Giants fan, I will *know* whether the Giants won or lost."

Another woman, marketing director for a medical supply company in the West, says her interest in sports has helped her out a number of times. "A lot of men really do like to talk about sports," she says, "but a lot of them have wives who criticize them for watching too much football or playing too much golf. If you're sympathetic to them and let them know you like to see a football game now and then too, all of a sudden you become a real person."

Some women also use sports language effectively and comfortably. Representative Barbara B. Kennelly of Connecticut commented on Geraldine Ferraro's Vice Presidential candidacy this way: "Working on legislation is one hit at a time, but the nomination was a home run." Although men will easily accept and appreciate a woman who effectively uses sporting terms, misusing them is a sure way for a woman to be ridiculed. She will only make it clear to everyone that she is an outsider, wishing to be part of the club but not knowing quite how.

A WOMAN'S MANNER AND STYLE

Women and men not only talk about different topics, they differ in the way they speak. That's a phenomenon anthropologists and linguists have observed and documented throughout various cultures and across decades.

In 1975 linguist Robin Lakoff wrote a book that changed the way many people saw male and female conversational patterns. The characteristics of "women's language," described in her book *Language and Woman's Place,* have been widely reported and have stimulated other researchers to examine linguistic differences between the sexes. Lakoff says women's language is almost different enough from men's to be a separate dialect. She says it is, above all, polite and tentative, rather than direct and informative.

Women use words that are almost absent from men's vocabulary. For example, women use precise descriptions for colors ("mauve," "ecru"). They use adjectives like "adorable," "cute," "charming," "sweet," "lovely," and "divine," which are rarely spoken by men.

Various studies show that in normal conversation men are likely to offer opinions, suggestions, information, and disagreement, all of which are assertions of status, whereas women tend to bridge the distance between themselves and others by being friendly and agreeable and by asking for information and opinions.

A typical conversation—and miscommunication—might go like this:

She: Would you like some help with that project?
He: Okay.
She: Well, if you don't really need it, just say so. I have plenty to do. I just thought you might want some of my material.
He: I said *okay.* What's your problem?

Her problem is that she expected some enthusiasm, some friendliness, maybe even a "Gee, thanks." He thought he had conveyed his willingness to accept help and didn't realize more was expected.

Men and women also use different emphasizers, with men using stronger ones than women. "Oh, dear, the elevator is broken again" is a sentence likely to be heard from a woman; a man is more apt to say, "Damn, the elevator is broken again."

Another characteristic of women's language is the use of "so" as an intensifier, as in "I'm *so* angry." "So" serves as a hedge on the statement, making it sound as if the speaker dare not say just how angry she is. Speaking in italics is another way women have of being extremely ladylike; emphasizing words, as if they were italicized, tells the listener how you want him to respond. That gives the impression the speaker is afraid of not being listened to, afraid her words won't have any impact.

In conversation women also are more likely than men to use questions. That's done either by adding "tag questions" to the end of statements ("The file is in the conference room, isn't it?") or by turning declarative sentences into questions with a rising intonation at the end ("The file is in the conference room?"). Both techniques make the speaker sound unsure of herself, as if she doesn't expect the listener to accept what she says. They also give the speaker an out if the listener disagrees; it's another way of hedging, another indication that the speaker is not fully confident of what she's saying. Neither is as strong as a direct question ("Is the file in the conference room?") or a statement ("The file is in the conference room").

Women also use tag questions to elicit conversation ("This elevator breaks all the time, doesn't it?"), again revealing a fear that the listener isn't interested enough to respond without a tug.

Other hedges, such as "I think," "I wonder," "I guess," "you know," "like," "kind of," and "well," indicate the speaker is unsure of her ideas and afraid of imposing her opinions on others. The constant use of questions and hedging phrases robs the speaker of any authority and gives the impression that she is apologizing for expressing opinions at all.

Although those characteristics describe a style of speaking that is more often used by women than by men, it is not exclusively female, nor are women bound to use it. One study, conducted at a police station, found that men use women's language when they are in a submissive role. Anyone who came into the police station, male or female, used women's language more than the police personnel did.

Women's language is the language of the powerless; because women frequently feel and often *are* less powerful than men, they tend to use less powerful language. But they don't have to.

Research has shown that women can gain more power simply by changing the way they speak. Anthropologist William O'Barr of Duke University and some colleagues taped weeks of criminal trials in North Carolina to find patterns in speech and language in the courtroom. Listening to the tapes, they noticed that a powerless style of speaking was used by many witnesses. The characteristics are like those Robin Lakoff observed in women's speech. O'Barr noted that some witnesses used language that involved frequent use of hedges ("I think" and "perhaps"), intensifiers ("very" and "so"), and rising intonation at the end of statements, turning them into questions. Other witnesses spoke more powerfully.

To find out what effect seemingly minor differences in language could have on jurors, O'Barr took part of the courtroom transcript and rewrote some of the testimony removing the hedges, intensifiers, and questioning tones. He then made four tapes using a woman and a man each speaking in the original powerless language and each in the rewritten, cleaned-up language.

On the original transcript a witness was asked, "What was the nature of your acquaintance with her?" The response was: "We were, uh, very close friends. Uh, she was even sort of like a mother to me."

Rewritten to be a powerful answer that response became: "We were close friends. She was like a mother to me."

In a test of mock jurors O'Barr found that everyone rated the powerful speaker—whether male or female—as more convincing, competent, intelligent, and trustworthy than the powerless speaker. Those are all characteristics women at work—as well as on the witness stand—want. Eliminating the powerless tics from her speech can help a woman seem more powerful.

Speak Firmly and Use Detail

Women also will be more successful if they rely on facts and rationale in their conversations with men. Women learn to trust their feelings and the information they gather through the subtle signals others throw out. They often don't see any reason to support intuition with rational argument. A man, however, is more comfortable hearing the facts. One man, for instance, who served on a government commission with a woman, expressed continual frustration with her refusal to support her decisions and viewpoints in debate with him. "She tended to take the position, 'Well, this is just the right thing to do' and wouldn't allow her conclusions to be subject to scrutiny. Her favorite line was 'I don't have to justify my opinion to you.' " Maybe she didn't need to explain herself, but he needed to hear it. A woman who wants to elicit more cooperation from men needs to make those adjustments in her language style.

Jerie McArthur says that because men rely on rationale, women need to talk to them that way. She says, for example, that if she discovered, through subtle signals such as tone of voice and how she felt around him, that someone was her political enemy, she would never try to convince another man of it unless she could cite specific detail: "Here's the specific behavior the man used, here's what he said, and therefore it appears he's not with us on this issue." With another woman she might need fewer specifics because of that "shortcut in communication"—the use of an emotional wavelength—that Jane Alexander and many other women have experienced with their own sex.

Men also use facts and detail to display power. At a luncheon meeting to explain his organization and its position on pending legislation, the male president of a national real estate trade group dominated conversation and kept himself the focus of attention. He frequently made points about the national economy by using specific numbers and complicated mathematical formulas that were impossible to follow. When conversation turned to more casual chitchat over dessert, he continued to dominate. Trading personal stories about stock investments, one of the guests made a joke about inheriting ¼ share in some stock. The group president came back with: "Well, when it split 2,500 to 1 you then had eight shares." At that point, one of the women present expressed awe at his ability to do calculations in his head. He laughed and answered, "The secret is to speak firmly and use detail." Apparently, being firm and specific is even more important than being accurate.

HOW MEN CONTROL CONVERSATIONS

The old stereotype of the gabby woman and the taciturn man doesn't hold up. Study after study of people in mixed-sex pairs and groups and of people in various occupations show that men speak more often and at greater length than women do. Studies show that some women, in all-female groups, try to achieve dominance over other women through talkativeness, but these same women keep mum in the presence of men. Through sheer volume of talk, men manage to control conversations.

There are some obvious advantages to monopolizing a conversation: You get your ideas across, you make sure the topics you want to discuss are talked about, and—an additional advantage—others are more likely to perceive you as a leader.

Killing topics of conversation that women introduce is another way men control talk. Sociologist Pamela Fishman studied sex differences in conversation and found that women work harder in conversations than men do. Women use strategies to try to get their topics introduced that men don't (or don't need to). In her study, for example, women asked questions three times as often as men did and often used attention-getters like "Guess what?" and "Did you know?" They also said "you know" ten times more than men did. Perhaps it's that behavior that gives women the reputation for

being garrulous. Despite their effort, the topics women tried to introduce were pursued only 36 percent of the time; men succeeded
96 percent of the time in getting their topics pursued.

How do men do it? One easy way is simply to give no response,
no encouraging "Is that so?" or "Then what?" or even a paltry
"Uh-huh." Women thereupon either drop a particular topic or stop
talking altogether. By being silent when talk is expected, men convey
disdain and lack of interest. They manipulate silence and take the
dominant role.

Men may not be deliberately controlling a conversation when they
respond in those meager ways to a woman's comments, however.
It may be that the man is simply signaling his attention in a way a
woman never would and in a way she doesn't expect from others.
Males indicate their attention with fewer nonverbal cues. Women
tend to return frequent encouraging cues—head nods, murmurs,
facial expressions—to keep the talker going. They also look at the
speaker more, both in mutual gazes and when he's not looking at
her.

If a man is failing to respond, a woman needs to find out whether
it's lack of attention or merely his different listening style. (Often
the direct question, "Do you want to hear about this?," will do.)
In addition, women who want to control a few conversations of their
own should learn to curb their enthusiastic responses. By handing
out fewer encouraging murmurs and by sometimes sitting silently
while *his* conversational topic drops, a woman can take a dominant
role.

COMPETITIVE MAN TALK

Men aren't always passive and laconic in their conversation, of
course. They have another conversational style that can be equally
confusing to women. It is an aggressive, competitive style used
particularly when other men are present. It can leave a woman won-
dering whether she'll ever get a word in.

In the female culture and in polite society, conversation proceeds through orderly turn-taking, with each speaker waiting for the other to signal readiness to give up the floor. A more dominant—and masculine—style is to take turns by interruption. At a business meeting, when men are engaged in competitive turn-taking, they grab the floor by butting in and grabbing a turn. According to Jerie McArthur, when they are engaged in this pattern they tend to listen to just the first half of a sentence in order to figure out what to say themselves. That's how they keep up the competitive pace of the conversation. "If you listen to the whole sentence," says McArthur, "then there's a split second in time before you can think of what to say and leap in. In those situations, women often find themselves thinking, 'There must be something wrong with me because I can't keep up with them; they're so much faster.' No, they're just listening differently."

Women who have been taught to be ladylike and polite and never interrupt anybody are at a disadvantage in business situations, where this competitive turn-taking goes on. A woman sitting politely, waiting her turn, will never be heard—and the men will think it's because she hasn't anything to say. Says Madelyn Jennings, senior vice president at the Gannett Company, "If you're in a meeting and don't open your mouth, you may not see them but there are black marks going up next to your name." Jennings says the old cliché about strong, silent men still applies: "A man can be considered deep," she says, "but a woman is considered inadequate in the same circumstances."

Through interruptions, men violate the conventional rules of conversation and assert their dominance. Candace West and Donald Zimmerman, sociologists at the University of California, Santa Barbara, found in mixed-sex groups that males interrupt females more than they interrupt other males and more than females interrupt anyone.

In a later paper following that research, West and Zimmerman compared the results of their study with similar data from parent-child conversations. They found "striking similarities between the pattern of interruptions in male-female interchanges and those observed in the adult-child transactions."

Men don't blatantly trample the rights of women speakers. West and Zimmerman point out that there are social constraints that keep any speaker from misusing a conversational partner—even a child —too severely. If a person does, he's labeled rude, domineering, or authoritarian. Interruptions are more subtle and—to the working woman—more lethal than that. The tendency of males to interrupt females implies, according to the researchers, that women's turns at talk are expendable and that women can be treated conversationally as "nonpersons."

West and Zimmerman contend that the use of interruptions by males is both a *display* of dominance or control and *in fact* a controlling device, because the incursions disorganize the flow, as the following conversation adapted from their research conspicuously demonstrates.

> *She:* How's your paper coming?
> *He:* All right, I guess. I haven't done much in the past two weeks.
> *She:* Yeah. I know how that can . . .
> *He:* Hey, got an extra cigarette?
> *She:* Oh, uh, sure. Well, like my paper . . .
> *He:* How about a match?
> *She:* Here you go. Uh, like *my* paper . . .
> *He:* Thanks.
> *She:* I was gonna tell you my . . .
> *He:* Hey, I'd really like to talk but I gotta run.
> *She:* Yeah.

Clearly, women who permit men to treat them in such a manner at work will have difficulty gaining credibility and will be at a grave disadvantage. But it doesn't have to be that way. Women don't have to speak "women's language"—and men's language isn't for men only.

Many women, especially powerful ones, use what's considered a male style of talking without thinking about it; they use it not because it's "men's language" but because it's the language of the dominant. Women sometimes unconsciously adapt their language to the situation, shifting from female patterns to male patterns, depending on the circumstances. One study, for example, showed that women talked significantly less with a male partner in a typical discussion, but when told they would be judged on their leadership abilities they talked equally with men and women.

The difference between the way the sexes talk has more to do with expectations and with dominance than with gender. Even differences in pitch are wider than anatomy demands. Anatomy accounts for a slightly higher pitch in female voices, but the expectation that male voices are low, and female ones high, exaggerates the difference. Women not only use higher pitches than men do, they use a greater range of them, which both men and women interpret as indications of emotion.

Without a doubt, traditional female speech patterns can get a working woman in trouble. Mostly they can keep her from exercising her full power. If, for example, at a meeting a woman uses questioning, tentative language, saying, "Don't you think we should take this action?" and a man responds, "Yes, we should take that action," others will go away thinking he made the contribution because he stated it in a definite way. A woman doesn't need to abandon her personal style (unless it's an overly cautious and tentative one); she can, however, learn dominant language patterns, which will make her sound more confident and powerful. *Feeling* and *being* more powerful will also change the way a woman sounds. A woman, too, can "speak firmly and use detail."

3 BODY LANGUAGE: TALKING TO MEN WITHOUT WORDS

David Givens, a research anthropologist at the University of Washington, teaches classes in nonverbal communication. For each class he gives his students the assignment to take their notebooks out into the field and write down all their observations of nonverbal signals given by others over a certain period of time. "Women bring back full notebooks," he says. "The men sometimes bring back an excuse: 'I didn't see anything.' "

It is well documented that women are more aware of body language than men and are better able to bring those observations to a conscious level. "Men aren't nearly as observant," says Givens. "Women can interpret the cues and know much more about what the social relationships are in the office, such as who likes whom. It's nonconscious most of the time, but they can give a pretty good interpretation of the social world."

Women often make use of the subtle information they pick up. Studies indicate, for example, that women show evidence of monitoring male partners and adapting their nonverbal behavior to the man's. Women also have been found to be more submissive nonverbally with males who score high on dominance tests and to behave in a more dominant way with males who test more submissive. Other studies show that girls—even infants—are better than boys at matching the emotional responses of others as indicated by facial expression.

Most of what we communicate nonverbally, through facial expression, tone of voice, body position, and gesture is not conscious. We don't necessarily know what messages we are sending and others don't consciusly interpret them. If a woman learns to bring that information to her awareness, however, her sensitivity to peripheral information and her skill in reading the emotion behind facial expression, tone of voice, body movement, and gesture can serve her well in the business world.

HIS AND HER BODY LANGUAGE

Nonverbal communication isn't neatly divided into male and female behaviors. Cultural, regional, and national patterns are confounding factors that affect how a signal will be interpreted or given. Southerners, for instance, smile more than Yankees. The Italians and the French gesture more than the British. And South Americans and Arabs stand closer together when talking than Americans do. Nonetheless, the differences in how the sexes in our country typically express themselves nonverbally are great. Some variations are familiar and obvious, others more subtle. If a person walks into a room, sits down with knees wide, arms stretched along the top of the sofa, and body tilted, would you guess it's a man or a woman? Even the least observant among us is likely to recognize that as male behavior. Whether you've thought about it or not, you know that men spread out, stressing width, when sitting and standing. Men also expose, even thrust forward, their crotch area when sitting, whereas women keep theirs closed or covered, even when wearing trousers. In their body movements, men stress gestures that move away from their bodies. Women keep themselves more compact, knees and arms close, back straight, gestures inward. When with other females, some women do spread their bodies more, but when face-to-face with men, one of the unspoken rules of body position is that the man's body is wider than the woman's.

Women also articulate their fingers, hands, and wrists more when they gesture. But generally they move less than men do. Females also look at others more, have a better facility for remembering faces, and match expressions in an empathetic way with others. Females —girls and women—tend to stand closer together when talking and to face one another more directly than males do. Even when instructed in studies to withhold approval, women smile and nod more than men.

Men and women differ in body movement in any number of curious ways. Females, for example, open and close their eyes more slowly and more intermittently than males. Nobody knows whether some of these differences have any meaning or significance. Some may have developed simply as ways for members of our species and culture to distinguish between the sexes.

The primary differences between the body language of males and females, however, is that women demonstrate more affiliative behavior, conveying warmth and expressiveness. Men use behavior indicating status and dominance. And that fact does have great significance for women working with men.

Dominance Gestures Are Male Gestures

Typical high-status, power gestures are those that show relaxation and aggressiveness at the same time. People with status can afford to be relaxed; subordinates usually keep a closed position with bodies contracted, clothing tidy and buttoned up, and postures rigid, indicating fearfulness. In a group, for example, a speaker with high status will lean back in a chair with hands linked behind the head or neck, body in an asymmetrical position taking up maximum space. Other power gestures and positions are sitting with a leg over the arm of a chair, straddling a chair backward, sitting with feet on a desk, touching fingertips in a steeple position, frowning, pointing, touching another person, and crowding someone else's space.

Some of these behaviors are simply not open to women—especially business women. Whether dressed in trousers or not, few can effectively straddle a chair backward or throw a leg over a chair arm. And few women in power positions use such movements—they're more likely to bring ridicule on a woman than status. To gain power, women can't merely imitate the aggressive gestures of men, but they can learn to use the status gestures that are available to them.

Women can, for example, exert power by relaxing in a man's office, by extending herself into his territory by leaning on his desk, crowding him, spreading her possessions, such as papers and work materials, in his areas and touching his belongings. She also can— occasionally and carefully—use the trivializing gestures that women (and children) are often subjected to, such as pats on the head or a finger touched to the other person's nose.

Women also can learn to read the power gestures of men and to avoid matching a man's dominance gestures with submissive ones. When a man exhibits aggression or dominance by crowding a woman's space, for example, she doesn't have to yield; and she doesn't have to smile when he frowns or lower her eyes when he stares. Such submissive nonverbal responses reinforce the higher status and power of men.

MORE AND BIGGER IS BETTER

One of the fundamentals of nonverbal communication is that the more status someone has, the more space they control. Dominant people are free to move in the territory of others (the boss, for instance, is free to walk into a subordinate's office); they are accorded more space for their bodies (no one crowds too close to the top brass around a meeting table or in the hallways); and the space they control is better, more desirable space (the corner office with a view goes to someone with power, the small one near the elevator goes to a subordinate). High-status people even take up more space with their signatures than the less privileged.

Dominant people—just like dominant animals—are more likely to be bigger than others as well. It doesn't just seem as if the executive offices and board rooms are filled with men who wear 42-long suits; indeed they are. Tall men are more likely to get jobs and promotions and are even paid more than short ones. We are so used to giving status and power to tall and big people that we assume important people are tall when they are not.

Where does the "bigger is better" maxim leave women, who are generally smaller than even an average-size man and certainly smaller than the six-footers who populate the upper ranks of business? It leaves them in a better position than might be imagined. The rules governing what's expected of men don't necessarily apply to women. In fact, women who have made it to executive and high-level positions are just as likely to be small or average as tall. Perhaps that's because small and average-size women meet the expectations of men (who are doing the promoting) and, perhaps, those women are less threatening than big women.

Women can use the tricks that average-size men employ to seem taller. A woman can elevate her body by standing to make a point or standing when others are seated; she can seem taller if she keeps her chin up and occasionally puts her hands behind her back so that she appears to be looking down on others.

Successful small women simply don't let their size become an issue or an impediment. "I've never considered it a problem," says one woman who has held executive positions and who is just over five feet tall. "I'm more aware of the terrible handicaps very tall women have had. Any number of them have told me of the troubles they had in grammar school and high school. I was spared that and was not as awkward with boys. Even if you're short you can dominate with power, intellect, and personality." Women of any size can, in addition, use touch to dominate, but they must do so with care and forethought, because touch is perhaps the most potent of all nonverbal signals.

TOUCH AND POWER

Although touch has many meanings and uses (particularly in intimate relationships), in the business world there is one governing principle: Touching privileges are part of the dominance hierarchy. The higher the status of a person, the more touching privileges she or he has. Psychologist Nancy Henley, who has written extensively on nonverbal behavior, theorizes that whether a touch is reciprocal lends significant meaning to the message. When a touch is reciprocated, it indicates a warmth and closeness; when it cannot or is not intended to be returned, it conveys status and power.

Study after study shows that touch affects the power balance by enhancing the power of the toucher and diminishing that of the recipient—no matter what their initial status relationship had been. Thus, a subordinate who touches a superior can gain status—or err seriously. One highly placed executive woman tells of the time she blundered with touch. She was walking to the board room with her CEO (a man), who was exuberant over some coup she had performed. He was in a terrific mood and threw his arm around her shoulder, giving her a hearty pat. Without thinking, she responded in what was to her a natural way: She wrapped her arm around his waist. "He froze," she reports. "I thought he was going to drop dead."

Her behavior was absolutely prohibited; because he had higher rank he could touch her, but her return touch was an affront and an act of insubordination.

Because touch has such potency as a dominance signal, it can be used to gain status over superiors and colleagues, but such uses should be deliberate rather than spontaneous. And certainly any power play against someone as strong as a CEO had better be meticulously thought out.

Touching Men

Touch usually contains a certain amount of ambiguity. The circumstances under which it occurs, the relationship between the people involved, and the intention of the toucher all influence the message. But touches between a man and a woman are tinged with confounding signals that complicate the situation.

For one thing, men don't always construe the same message from a touch that women might. Women cannot assume men will respond the same way to touch that a woman would. Psychologist Brenda Major, who has researched and written about gender patterns in touching, reports that studies show men and women both respond positively to the touch of an obviously higher-status person, presumably because they see the touch as appropriate to the role. However, when the status of the toucher and the touched are equal or ambiguous, women usually respond positively to being touched, but men are either neutral or negative, especially if the toucher is female.

A study of the effects of a female nurse's touch on male and female patients undergoing elective surgery illustrates that point. Women touched by the nurse reported considerably less anxiety about surgery and had lower blood pressure in the recovery room afterward than women who weren't touched. On the other hand, men who were touched reported more anxiety than those who were not and had higher blood pressure in the recovery room than men who weren't touched.

Major speculates that the reason may have been that the women were more likely to see the nurse as being either of higher or equal status, but the men may have seen her as of lower status. Another interpretation is that men are more attuned to the dominance cues of touching (rather than the warmth that also might be intended) and thus are more sensitive to the perceived put-down of being touched. Women may be more aware of the warmth message in the touch, even when it comes from a lower-status person.

A woman can subject a man to a great deal of discomfort by touching him in ways he finds inappropriate, which is something a woman can use—carefully—to her advantage. A woman, for example, might be wise to avoid making her boss uncomfortable, but touch can be used to control the behavior of a colleague.

A junior high school teacher, for example, was frequently made uncomfortable by the touches of one of the other teachers, a male physical education instructor. "It wasn't sexual—I knew that much —but it still made me squirm," she says. "He would casually place a hand on my shoulder (easy to do since he was about eight inches taller) and look down at me." Had that woman been wise to the ways of power touching, she would have known that he was probably threatened by her in some way (or simply was a man who enjoyed and expected to have status over women). In any case she could have unbalanced him by sending a few dominance signals of her own with touch. She might have, for example, taken an opportunity to place her hand on his shoulder when he was seated at his desk (perhaps adding a little zinger like "How are we coming on the first-quarter grades?").

Touch Can Seem, If Not Be, Sexy

A second complicating element in touch between men and women is that any touch has the potential for a sexual intent or interpretation.

"Touching is a very primitive form of communication—the most primitive of all," says anthropologist David Givens. "When you touch a person it goes right to the emotional centers and sometimes gets misinterpreted. A man may feel the touch is more serious than a woman intended." Because of that primitive power, Givens advises men and women, but especially women, to be very careful about the touching they do at work. "Touch is fine for camaraderie among your own sex," he says, "but when you do it between sexes, men tend to misunderstand." Even a casual touch on the arm is a potent form of communication.

The widespread confusion over what touches between the sexes mean was obvious during the Walter Mondale/Geraldine Ferraro campaign for the Presidency, which was the first time a woman had run with a man on the national ticket. Much fuss was made in the press and among campaign advisers about whether Mondale could or should touch Ferraro during public appearances. If so, how and where and what would people think? If not, how would they show their solidarity, and would they seem not to be a team? During the Carter/Mondale campaign the two men frequently embraced, as male running mates always have. In the traditional political campaign pose, running mates stand facing their audience, with one arm around the other's waist and with the outside arm raised in triumph. So far, no one has suspected male candidates who use that pose of being homosexual. And yet any touch between a man and a woman contains the possibility of sexuality.

Women who work with men usually find there are some who cannot, under any circumstances, be touched. They simply are not comfortable with a woman's touch, whatever her status. Over time, and through effort in getting to know the men she works with, a woman comes to know which ones she can touch and which she must keep her hands 'off. Women also learn which men she will permit to touch her. One young MBA who works almost exclusively with men says there is a group of male colleagues she works closely with who touch one another and her freely. They even trade back rubs at the end of difficult days. Men in a power clique above her, however, never touch her and she never touches them. "I wouldn't want them to," she says. "They don't respect me in the way the others do."

The more women touch men in business situations—with handshakes, reassuring shoulder pats, a restraining or let's-go hand on an arm, even hugs shared in moments of victory—the less opportunity men will have to use touch to dominate women and the less firmly touch will be associated with sex. Touch is too important a means of exerting status and building solidarity among colleagues for women to be denied the use of it.

WHAT'S COURTSHIP DOING IN THE OFFICE?

Touch isn't the only nonverbal behavior that brings sex into the office. So does a subtle—and pervasive—pattern of movements used unconsciously by men and women in almost all dealings with one another.

Termed "quasi-courtship" behavior, it was first observed twenty years ago by Albert Scheflen, professor of psychiatry at Albert Einstein College of Medicine in New York, who was studying different methods of psychotherapy. His observations of patients and therapists revealed that behavior is patterned and systematic. One of the patterns that invariably appeared was very like American courtship.

Further study indicated that the behavior occurs anywhere men and women come together, including the workplace. It is characterized by high muscle tone resulting in an erect torso, disappearance of sagging and bagginess in face and body. Eyes brighten and, Scheflen suggests, changes in body odor may even occur. Preening usually goes along with these changes too. Women stroke their hair, check makeup in a mirror, rearrange their clothing. Men comb or stroke their hair, button and adjust coats, and pull up socks. The couple participating turn their bodies toward one another and engage in flirtatious glances, hold one another's gaze, use demure gestures and head-cocking. Women cross their legs and expose a portion of thigh, place a hand on a hip, display the wrist or palm, and stroke the thigh or wrist with fingers.

It sounds as if it would be impossible to get any work done with all this flirting going on, but Scheflen says that this behavior is always accompanied by some moderating behavior that lets the participants know that the intention is not sexual. There may, for example, be some reference, usually nonverbal, to the inappropriateness of the setting for courtship. (Eyes might roll toward others in the room to emphasize that the couple is not alone, for instance.)

Anthropologist Givens followed up Scheflen's work, adding through his own research to the list of courtship behaviors. He says that today the same basic relationship exists. ''When you have men and women together there's always going to be courtship cues,'' he says.

A woman executive, for example, used nonsexual courtship cues with a male subordinate she had called into her office to discuss a project. When he sat down she quite unconsciously touched her neck, adjusted her skirt, and crossed her legs. He responded by shifting to face her, hiking up his socks, and then leaning forward with his elbows rested on his knees. The office setting, the status difference between the pair, and the lack of sexual intent keep such behavior from detracting from the business at hand and, in fact, smooth the way by relaxing and putting both at ease.

Some important aspects of courtship and quasi-courtship behavior are meekness and submissive cues, which include rounded and el-

evated shoulders, chest caved in, feet rotated inward, head tilted.
Men as well as women use such behavior in real courtship so as not
to intimidate or scare off the other. When the same cues are used at
work, however, they bring different results for men and women.

Women who use meekness cues so effectively in courtship can
unwittingly sabotage their efforts at work by using the same signals.
They risk appearing submissive and weak. Men are not in the same
danger of losing power in a business situation with courtship behavior. One advantage they have, according to Givens, is that their
clothing helps cover up meekness. Their suit jackets and lapels make
their chests look bigger, shoulder pads give them width. (When men
are truly courting they generally take off that power uniform so as
not to intimidate women.)

Many very persuasive men use quasi-courtship cues as part of their
personal style. "Anwar Sadat, for example, gave off a lot of courtship
cues; he did a lot of head tilting, smiling, shoulder gesturing," says
Givens. "Phil Donahue does the same thing—lots of pitching and
rolling of shoulders and head tilts—courting the guests on his show.
It's all a part of charisma."

That's part of male charisma, anyway. It may be to the advantage
of very powerful men—like Ronald Reagan, who shrugs and grins
and ducks his head in an almost coquettish manner—to diffuse some
of their power so as not to threaten others, but women seldom have
a surplus of power. Women high up in a business heirarchy can
sometimes effectively use courtship gestures and the submissive cues
that go along with them, but those further down the ladder are better
off curbing that behavior and opting for a more neutral style that
doesn't force them to give up any of their authority.

What a Smile Reveals

Smiles are an essential aspect of the courtship pattern. But smiling
is also a nonverbal cue with multiple uses and interpretations, many
of which have nothing to do with amusement, pleasure, or humor.
It's often a gesture of appeasement or submission offered upward in

the status hierarchy. Smiles also signal nervousness, apology, greeting, and, when used with angry words, they can soften the negative effect of the message. They also can be used to seek approval. And they are used much more often by females than males.

Smiles that come too freely and in inappropriate situations often indicate uncertainty and discomfort. Nervous, mirthless smiling and laughing can become a habit. Once you become aware of it, you'll see it and hear it, especially from women, wherever you go.

At a recent press conference in New York, representatives from a drug company and several research physicians reported in a panel discussion on a new vaccine developed by the company. The discussion was serious and probing because the vaccine had the potential for wide use among children. Reporters asked tough questions about how research on the drug was conducted and what the side effects were. The sole woman on the panel, the firm's marketing director, smiled throughout the discussion. On the few occasions when a joke was made to ease the tension in the room, either by a reporter or panelist, the woman laughed loudest and longest. Her behavior was not only inappropriate, but conveyed precisely what she wanted to hide: her nervousness, discomfort, and fear.

Women smile not only to cover up disturbing feelings, but often to put others at ease, to encourage others, to fill gaps in conversation, and to create a relaxed and comfortable atmosphere. Those smiles can be very useful in business.

Researchers have documented that women smile 17 percent of the time when they're listening; men smile less than 8 percent of the time. Because women smile easily and often, the dearth of smiles from men can be confusing to women. There's no indication that men are necessarily feeling less friendly or attentive, but to a woman they certainly seem to be.

The Meaning of Gazes

Women do more of the looking, too. They hold gazes, both ones that are returned and those that are not, longer and more often. It's a pattern that's established in infancy and carries throughout life. When speaking, women look at the listener (though not necessarily meeting the eyes of that person) almost 60 percent of the time; men gaze less than 40 percent of the time. In general, gazing is an instance in which the female pattern follows that of the nondominant and the male follows that of the higher-status person. Low-status people are generally more vigilant; they need to monitor the behavior of the higher-status person to know how to behave, and to know what others are up to. The higher your status, the less looking you have to do.

People tend to look more at those they feel good about and at those they're expecting or hoping for approval from. And usually, people look more when listening than when talking. That's because when you're talking you have to think about what you're saying and don't want the distractions of the listener; for the listener, however, it can be useful to watch the speaker, because you can pick up nonverbal cues that will contribute to the verbal message.

Looking isn't always a low-status behavior, however. It is used in two ways to show dominance. The stare is a powerful device for establishing dominance; the one who diverts a gaze when stared at is the less dominant. And not looking when someone is speaking can reinforce the superiority of the listener.

One of the most basic of nonverbal signals, looking has many interpretations. It can signal a desire to approach or interact (which is sometimes why a stranger's gaze causes discomfort); it can indicate an intention to attack, or it can show interest and longing. Diverting a gaze during conversation can indicate embarrassment or guilt or lack of attention, which is probably where the notion that eye contact is desirable came from.

Some women may have carried it too far, however. A woman can make a man uneasy with too much looking. She can come across, especially in a business situation, as too intense and earnest. A man won't know why he feels uncomfortable around a woman who looks at him continually (or more than a man would look at him), but he will be disturbed. Because men tend to conceal their feelings, however, gazing may be one of the few ways women can get information crucial to them about men's thoughts and behavior. In addition to what can be learned from watching specific behavior, women can learn a lot about a man by studying his face (preferably when he doesn't know she's looking!).

HOW MUCH CAN A FACE SAY?

In the 1984 Summer Olympic games, American cyclist Connie Carpenter pulled just inches ahead of another American biker in the final moments of the road race to win a gold medal. Her husband, Davis Phinney, a member of the men's cycling team, was in the crowd at the finish line to greet her. Later a television reporter asked Carpenter what was the first thing Phinney said to her after the race. She replied: "He said with his face, 'How did you do?' and I mouthed, 'I think I won.'"

We often are able to interpret specific messages delivered with facial expressions by people we know well. But even with acquaintances and strangers we sometimes can do the same. A frown, for example, indicates we've overstepped some boundary, and a look of doubt from a boss says an idea wasn't well received.

Without deliberate intention, people can assert dominance with a facial expression. A study of preschool children revealed that even at that age children are equipped to assert dominance or submission in appropriate situations. The researcher found that in competitive play the children telegraphed their expectations of the outcome with a "win face" or "loss face." And they were very accurate with their predictions. The win face—raised brows, wide-open eyes, jutting neck, and raised chin, which is similar to dominance expressions in lower primates—was shown by the winner in two-thirds of the encounters. The loss face, shown in more than half the loss situations, was furrowed brow, squinted eyes, retracted neck, and lowered chin. All the children, boys and girls, showed those faces.

We can reveal our current emotional state and create impressions about ourselves with facial expressions. The difficulty for women, however, is that men tend to be less revealing about their emotions, and especially hide fear and sadness. The value of the stony face perfected by so many men, particularly in business situations, is that they keep information under control, often the very information others are eager to have, and thus maintain personal power. Certain types of men have been taught through cultural training to reveal nothing, above all to conceal any vulnerabilities.

One woman says the head of her company is a master of the stone face. "You don't know," she says, "whether he's going to explode in anger when you finish your presentation or praise you to the skies." Her defense has been to learn to deliver her ideas as coolly and calmly as possible, and to know ahead of time precisely what she wants to say. She knows she'll have to proceed through the entire presentation without a single cue from him.

When a man's face becomes suddenly stony, it usually means he's getting into territory that threatens him. An immobile face, narrowed eyes, and slit mouth on a silent man indicates he's in over his head. He doesn't know how to respond, except perhaps with an outburst, and he's trying to control that. If a woman sees that type of stone face, she knows that the man is upset and that she's not likely to get sensible behavior as a next move. Because she doesn't necessarily know what upset him, her best tactic is to back off and try another approach. His reticence and desire to keep his cool won't permit him to reveal what he's feeling. Although a man's mood is less likely to be divulged by his face than a woman's, his character and personality may be etched clearly in his features.

Reading Men's Faces

We get our facial structure from genes and family. What really makes a face individual, however, is not so much genetics and the features we are born with as life itself. "We build our faces by the experiences we have," says Narayan Singh Khalsa, a psychologist in private practice in California. "They create a road map formed by the most frequently experienced emotions.'' He likens our faces to topographical maps that reveal, to anyone who can read the signs, what we've been through. Over time, our faces settle in, taking on the expressions and emotions that have dominated our lives.

Khalsa, who uses face reading in his own practice and teaches his techniques to other therapists, interprets some typical male facial expressions as follows:

Thin lips indicate the man is withholding and very power-manifesting. He's the combative, determined, classic "male machine."

Jutting jaw indicates aggressiveness, along with the male machine characteristics.

Angular cheeks are another indication of a withholding man, who in addition is likely to be negative toward women. (That may add up to an attractive face, but one that could be difficult to work with.)

Eyes are often revealing. Puffiness under eyes indicates chronic grief, feeling alone, and lacking emotional support from others. Eyes with hollows beneath them also indicate loneliness, characteristic of what Khalsa calls the "urban hermit." Narrow eyes are indicative of someone who is suspicious and stingy; he's withholding information because he feels he's living in hostile territory and is unwilling to share anything. (With observation, you can distinguish between eyes that are naturally small and those that have narrowed through distrust.) Wide-open eyes, on the other hand, indicate someone who is understanding.

There are danger signs to watch for in older men's faces. Jowls, like those familiar on Richard Nixon, indicate a man has been holding a lot of anger in his jaw throughout life; the rage is still there, but the muscles have given up. Vertical lines down the face indicate fear; he's a lonely man who is afraid he'll do something wrong. He can be very difficult to work with because he has no trust in others; he considers himself to be living and working in a foxhole. Puffiness can indicate the man has endured and is enduring a lot of grief; it can also mean he's handling dependency feelings with alcohol.

Khalsa says that although being able to identify and decipher specific characteristics can be helpful, it's not as important as getting an overall reading on a face. Most faces are made up of a complicated blend of emotions that reveals subtle information.

You can practice face reading by examining photographs. Ask yourself, what would this person be saying with this expression on his face? What is his point of view? And, most important, what are your reactions to what you are seeing? What emotions does the face provoke in you?

GROWN-UPS DON'T SQUIRM

It is not enough for a working woman to be an astute interpreter of male nonverbal communication, she must also be skillful when it comes to controlling her own body language. She must remember that we all send and receive nonverbal signals unconsciously and continually. Even men, who are not as adept as women in bringing those messages to a conscious level, nonetheless receive impressions.

The image you want to convey with your body language is one of relaxed control. Too much movement is a sign of immaturity. Hands at the face and mouth, scratching the head, tapping fingers, and gesturing excessively are characteristic of adolescents; such gestures are not the purposeful movements of a mature person.

Typical "squirm gestures," as David Givens calls them, which signal stress, are biting lips or pressing them together, adjusting clothing, stroking face, neck, and back of head, and touching an earlobe. Those movements tend to have the same effect when used by men and women. Describing one of the men in her office who, although he is second in command, is widely regarded as lacking power and authority, a woman said: "He smiles or grimaces a lot and moves restlessly in his chair as you talk."

Too much movement in the speaker is equally distracting and women tend to use more gestures when speaking than men do. Perhaps that's because they tend to have less power than men and thus have reason to fear others aren't truly listening. One woman, with misplaced pride, is fond of saying, "People tell me I just couldn't talk if I sat on my hands." Her gestures, instead of having whatever charming effect she imagines, lend a kind of desperation to her conversation. Her hands insist the listener pay attention; what gains attention, however, is her insecurity. She distracts rather than captivates the listener. More powerful, confident speakers learn to let their words do the work.

Dorothy Gregg, who has held high-level executive positions in several companies, says she and the men she works with pay a lot of attention to body language. She says women learn quickly that top male executives carefully watch everything—but especially hands. "You learn to put your hands in your lap," she says, "because men are very distracted by the use of hands. They've learned a long time ago to control theirs. If you use your hands even modestly, they become absolutely fascinated by your hands and can't look at anything else."

Women can learn to use body language that conveys power and confidence. David Givens, at the University of Washington, consults with female executives both for his own research and as a business. He tells of the time a woman who was high up in her company came to him complaining that she was not being taken as seriously in meetings as she wanted. Givens videotaped her role-playing a meeting where she presented important ideas to people sitting across the table. Examining the tape he found that this woman continually used her body to take away authority from her words. For example, she leaned back with her arms wrapped at her waist, a self-consoling gesture; she tilted her head to one side, lifted her shoulders, and used a lot of shrug gestures when she presented facts. "Around the world, the shrug shows uncertainty," says Givens, "and she was shrugging as she gave her most important points. She was disclaiming her importance with her nonverbal performance." Because she felt intimidated around the board table, she gave off submissive cues.

Givens coached her to stop shrugging and tilting her head and he encouraged her to lean forward with her forearms on the table when she gave her presentations. Just by making those simple changes, she later reported, she gained authority and the confidence that came with being taken seriously. By monitoring their behavior, other women can do the same.

4 HOW MEN USE HUMOR

Daniela Kuper, owner of a Colorado advertising agency, was the only woman in a group gathered to hear a real estate developer describe a new project. She had been hired to do the advertising. The developer was pointing out locations and features on blueprints tacked to a large board at the front of the meeting room, when he paused at a hatched line stretched across the plans. "Daniela," he said, "that's where the choo-choo will go."

Two men laughed hard and long. They got the joke and agreed with its message: "Hey guys, there's a woman in our midst; we know women aren't too bright so I'll help her along." Two other men looked at her uncomfortably and tried sympathetic smiles. They got the joke too, but didn't share its message. The rest didn't notice anything had happened. The joke and its sting passed right by them. It didn't miss Kuper, of course, who has learned what a powerful tool—and weapon—humor can be in business dealings with men.

Humor in all its forms, including banter, wit, repartee, irony, cynicism, jokes, pranks, and ridicule, turns up at work sooner or later. We take it for granted, and because it's assumed to be fun we think it's not important. But it is. Humor performs significant social and psychological functions, and in relationships between men and women it can be of particular consequence. Men sometimes differ from women in the ways they use humor and how often they use it, and even in what they find amusing.

WHY HUMOR MATTERS

Almost everyone uses humor as one way of coping with problems, big and small, and it's as true on the job as it is in our personal lives. Stepping back from the seriousness of a situation and looking at the light side helps put difficulties in perspective. Humor performs other significant psychological functions too. It can make a person feel superior; by pointing out and laughing at the foibles, foolishness, and shortcomings of others we assure ourselves that we're not like that. The pleasure we get from seeing others ridiculed depends on who's being put down. And if you identify with the victor and have a negative view of the butt, as the men who laughed at Daniela Kuper did, you'll find the joke all the funnier.

Humor, especially if it results in laughter, can be a powerful tension-reliever. The conflicts and antagonisms that occur when people who have little personal attachment are thrust together—as on the job—are released with humor. Anthropologist A. R. Radcliffe-Brown wrote that in such circumstances the result is often a joking relationship, both friendly and antagonistic, where teasing and insults are permitted, but no one is allowed to take offense.

The ambiguity of humor is one of its principal attractions. Because a jest is often subtle and open to more than one interpretation, it can be used to communicate taboo interests and values, to probe for what another person is thinking, or to make a suggestion that the joker is not sure will be accepted.

Humor also can provide at least momentary freedom from the constraints of our adult roles; through jokes we can mention forbidden subjects, engage in offensive or childish behavior, and even step beyond the bounds of good taste. In the playful context of a joke every moral taboo can be violated—and if anyone challenges our behavior, we can always say, "I was only joking!"

Laughter can even have positive physical effects; recent research shows that a good laugh can have effects similar to moderate exercise. Strong laughter has relieved headaches and lowered blood pressure.

Laughter Draws Us Together

One of the most important functions of humor and laughter is the bond it can create between people, and that's why it can be especially useful at work. The urge to share a joke is almost irresistible. Although we can get pleasure from something humorous when alone, the pleasure is increased when it's shared. How and whether the joke is shared, in fact, is a more significant determinant of how much laughter goes on than the quality of the joke.

In his book *Humor: Its Origin and Development,* psychologist Paul McGhee reports a study of the responses children make to humor in social situations. For the experiment, groups of three children listened to humorous tapes through earphones. Two of the three were confederates in the study, the third was being observed for reactions. The amount the third child laughed depended not on the jokes, which remained consistent, but on how much eye contact the other two children made. The more they looked at each other—excluding the third child—the less the third child laughed, but when they began to look at the third child, that child laughed more. We don't need research to tell us that the same thing applies to adults. If a group of people are standing around the water cooler laughing at someone's wit or shenanigans, anyone who feels excluded from the group won't find any of it funny.

Those with whom we share a sense of humor help us define ourselves and help us to establish membership in groups. By laughing at what others are laughing at, we demonstrate that we share common likes, dislikes, ideas, and attitudes. Laughing at another's joke is a sign of acceptance; refusing to laugh indicates a rejection of the humorist, as well as those who are joining in the laughter.

Humor Also Divides Us

So important to our relationships is the ability to laugh together that not being able to share a joke can indicate a critical division. In *On Aggression,* Konrad Lorenz writes: "Laughter forms a bond and simultaneously draws a line. If you cannot laugh with the others, you feel an outsider, even if the laughter is in no way directed against yourself or indeed against anything at all."

Being unable to share a joke and the camaraderie it builds can cause serious problems for working people. If we don't laugh with those we work and do business with, we miss valuable opportunities to build goodwill.

Often the widest division between who's in on the joke and who's left out is that between men and women. The sexes don't necessarily find the same things funny, as many women in business have found. Laura, a young woman with an MBA from an Ivy League school, works for a large company in the entertainment business. Talking about the power group of men in her office, she says, "I never know how to please them. They are a rollicking, joke-a-minute kind of group. I think I can be a pretty funny person, but I sometimes walk out of the room thinking, 'I'm cracking up at my own jokes. Why isn't anybody else laughing?' Other times I walk out of there thinking, 'What *are* they laughing at?' It's so stupid and slapstick; it's not what I consider funny."

HIS AND HER HUMOR

The primary divider between what females and males find funny is a matter of aggression and hostility. Studies of children indicate that boys and girls show generally the same comprehension and appreciation of humor, with one significant difference—boys take more pleasure in hostile humor. Boys as young as four or five are more likely than girls to choose an aggressive cartoon as the funnier one, and boys' humor initiated during play tends to be more hostile than that of girls. According to psychologist McGhee, who has researched and written extensively about how humor develops, there's a "pervasiveness of hostility in boys' humor." When those boys grow up, they may refine their behavior, but they don't forget the lessons learned on the playground.

Sigmund Freud makes much of the use of humor as a release for aggression. He divides jokes into two types: innocent (those, like word plays, with no aim beyond themselves) and tendentious (those with a purpose). He classified tendentious jokes in four categories:

obscene, hostile (with an intention of aggressiveness, satire, or defense), cynical (critical and blasphemous), and skeptical. According to Freud, the only really funny jokes are those with a purpose: "The pleasurable effect of innocent jokes is as a rule a moderate one . . . A non-tendentious joke scarcely ever achieves the sudden burst of laughter which makes tendentious ones so irresistible." So irresistible to men, that is.

Venting Aggression—with a Smile

The reason men use more hostile humor is simple: Men have more aggression to release. And hostile jokes permit them to release it in a socially acceptable way.

Men often use aggressive humor with personal friends and business friends, but women usually don't. One man, for example, relentlessly needles a co-worker he's friendly with about the man's receding hairline. It's harder to picture a woman ridiculing a female colleague about her flabby thighs unless she were ready to end the friendship.

"Joking relationships between men can be very savage," says Dorothy Gregg, executive vice president, Research & Forecasts, a communications research firm. "If it were physical combat, one would be dead. The joking relationship gets so rough that it becomes quite appalling, even to the participants and to other men sitting around. At a meeting about costs with a CEO I've seen one executive vice president say jokingly to another, 'Oh, yes, and you lost that $40 million down in Mexico on that crazy investment.' He laughs at the end of the statement, but the circumstance wasn't a laughing matter to anyone else in the room or to the victim."

The hostile intent of humor is often deliberate. A male lawyer, whose office is almost exclusively male except for the female secretaries, says, "My humor is cynical, mocking. I use humor to get points across, to get on people's cases. I use humor to let someone know I'm pissed." Asked whether there's any other kind of humor going on at his workplace, the same man said, "There's a lot of teasing that goes on between the secretaries and the lawyers, but

that's just boss-secretary, man-woman stuff.'' Clearly, that humor
doesn't have the significance for him that the trenchant jesting he
uses with his peers does.

Contrast that view of humor with what Laura has to say about the
kind of joking she uses and enjoys on the job. She works closely
with a group of men she admires; they are men she says who are not
aggressive, nor particularly intent on making it to the executive suite.
Her relationship with them depends heavily on a shared sense of
humor. They make up parodies of Christmas carols at holiday time,
and when their boss got married they made up a song for her. The
power group in her firm—an all-male division that calls the shots
—would never take part in that sort of play. ''The other group,''
says Laura, ''uses much more guffaw, private-joke mumbling that
to me isn't communication. My humor is based on conjuring up an
image. If I say to you, remember on 'I Love Lucy' how she stuffs
the chocolates in her mouth? That's communication, that's saying,
'I have an image in my mind. Do you have the same image?' ''

What Laura is missing is that the power group are indeed com-
municating, but in a different way and with other needs in mind.

Men Will Be Boys

The power group of men at Laura's office are engaging in a primitive
kind of communication. They're grown-ups dressed in pinstripes,
but in some ways they're still boys, still relating to other males as
boys, and still considering girls to be no fun. Says one young man
who works in a retail business: ''If I were an employer, I would
include some women in a group of men workers to keep the men
from fooling around too much and not doing their jobs. When men
work together and form a group they get so they can act like little
boys around each other, which I think men do whenever they can.''

The boyish behavior comes out in many different ways. A female
manager tells about a group of four male computer programmers
who work under her. They're bright and friendly and well liked,
although they've formed a tight clique among themselves. Much of
their relationship is based on practical jokes. When a member of the

group goes on vacation he can be sure he'll return to some prank the others contrived. One came back to find every item on his bulletin board meticulously tacked upside down. Another couldn't get into his office: His chums had installed a partition blocking the door to his cubicle.

Although this type of joking has hostile elements, it's attenuated hostility, like the vigorous rough-and-tumble play of boys and the horseplay and friendly shoving so evident among men in beer commercials. Its purpose is not just to vent aggression, but to say, "Hey guys, I'm with you." Men are seldom comfortable saying what they feel, particularly with other men, but a joke or slap on the back can convey a positive message. And, most puzzling to women, so can an outrageous insult. "Ranking," the art of competitive, humorous insulting, is a favorite pastime of men. Through jokes, men may develop solidarity with other men without getting too close or having to put any emotions in words. It's behavior that necessarily excludes females—it's boy-to-boy, man-to-man interaction that has everything to do with bonding with other males and nothing to do with females. That's why Laura—and many other women like her—sometimes feel hopelessly left out of the joke. No matter how adept a woman is at working with men, no matter how strong her ties with them, she can't be one of the boys.

Experienced women learn to accept that. "I don't feel at all excluded when it occurs," says Dorothy Gregg, who has worked for years with men in high corporate positions. "I firmly believe it's not done against me. I've seen it ever since I was born. It's something men grow up practicing. It makes them happy, makes them feel close to each other. And I don't think you're going to stop men from doing it."

JOKING WITH MEN

Man-to-man joking isn't the only kind men use, however, and women aren't always left out. In fact, successful women are often known for a good sense of humor. "The women I know who get along best with men are those who have a wonderful facility to enter into a joking relationship with them,'' says Gregg. ''And that makes men feel comfortable.''

A woman who can respond with ease to the aggressive humor of a man in business is especially fortunate. Although men at times may be cautious when turning vicious humor on women, because they can't be sure how women will respond, they do it nonetheless. At best, a woman will respond in kind. ''Unless she can respond with something witty or a little bit funny that turns his comment off lightly, she's in deep trouble and it's an embarrassment to everybody,'' says Gregg. The worst response a woman can give is to take the comment too seriously. And yet that is often a woman's reaction—it's not easy to handle yourself when you're the target of a put-down or joking attack.

Countless women like Karen, who works for a large accounting firm, have been the targets of hostile humor. Karen joined a team of five, herself and four men, to solve a particular problem in the company. The work involved travel to several cities where the firm had offices and resulted in day after day of the team eating meals together and spending all working hours in each other's company. Throughout the trip, Karen felt the odd woman out; the men were all partners in the firm (she was not) and a couple of them were noticeably uncomfortable in her presence. They frequently shared jokes and asides that excluded her.

Near the end of the trip, Karen was making dinner conversation by talking about her plans to go to graduate school. Asked by one of the men, who had been especially uncomfortable with her, how she would find time to do that, she said she was considering a program with night classes. His response, delivered as a joke, went right to the heart of her greatest fears and vulnerabilities: ''What will you do? Put a picture of yourself on your kid's bedroom door?''

Her response was to excuse herself from the table and go to the women's bathroom where she had a long cry. She was too weary and too hurt to muster a comeback; and yet this was just the sort of situation that called for standing up to a man's hostile humor. Had she been able to, her best defense would have been to deflect the attack with a comment that concealed her pain. The object in such cases is to show you're *not* affected by the jab. She might have said, for instance, "No need—she's already got me on videotape telling her to brush her teeth and hang up her clothes." Or she might have lightly turned the attack back on the joker by saying something like: "Oh, is that what you do when you're on the road? I've been looking for some useful long-distance parenting tips."

Such responses serve important purposes. They avoid a woman's seeming meek and helpless in the eyes of her male colleagues—and in her own. They help her put a stinging remark in perspective; it is far less painful to turn away such a comment than to absorb it and feel the full impact. By responding with a comeback, a woman restores the balance of power between herself and the man who made a joke at her expense.

Although a man may expect a vicious joke to be turned aside and made into something light (while his point is driven home), few women have mastered or had an opportunity to learn the rough give-and-take of men's humor. Most women are not accustomed to being the joker, especially around the opposite sex.

Men Tell the Jokes, Women Do the Laughing

Beginning as early as the preschool years, distinctions turn up between the amount of joking that males and females use, with boys making more frequent attempts at humor. As early as age three, boys are more likely to act silly, make faces, and horse around than girls are. In the grade school years boys show more silly rhyming, naughty words, and playful talk than do girls.

Research on adults also indicates that, when it comes to humor, men give and women receive. Sociologist Rose Laub Coser conducted a study of the uses of humor among the staff of a mental hospital. She found that although females made up more than half the staff, they rarely initiated any humor. Of 103 witticisms observed in meetings, 99 were made by men. Women often laughed harder, however. Coser observed that many of the women frequently made witty remarks in informal situations. Their lack of joke-telling in formal meetings didn't reflect an inability, she contends, but the conformity to a social norm that says a woman with a good sense of humor is one who laughs, but not too loudly, when a man is witty or tells a joke.

The reasons women use humor less, at least around men anyway, are complex. Part of the explanation must lie, as Coser suggests, in the socialization females get toward passivity. Women also are expected to be the arbiters of manners and morality and, according to linguist Robin Lakoff, who wrote the book *Language and Woman's Place,* as such they can't also tell jokes. "Women don't tell jokes" is one of the conventions Lakoff says is associated with women. She says, "It is axiomatic in middle-class American society that, first, women can't tell jokes—they are bound to ruin the punchline, they mix up the order of things, and so on. Moreover, they don't 'get' jokes. In short, women have no sense of humor."

The close association of humor and aggression also contributes to making joke-telling more appropriate for males; for a woman to be a jester in a mixed-sex group means she must violate the norm that says females don't dominate males.

Another reason women may be the ones doing the laughing instead of the joking is that laughing at another's joke is an almost sure way to gain acceptance and approval. People who laugh at others' jokes are considered warm and friendly and are usually well liked. And women may have stronger motivations than men to seek affection and attention.

A woman who owns a public relations firm in New York City offers another explanation for what she observes as the greater use of humor by men in business: "Women are too intent on projecting a businesslike image. They still perceive everything they're involved in as a life-and-death situation. I think humor is one of the greatest undervalued and under-talked-about skills of management."

Another important reason, however, may involve differences in status and power between the sexes. Joking tends to be characteristic of the powerful. And witty, joking people are frequently viewed as being leaders, in their own eyes and by others.

HUMOR FLOWS DOWNWARD

Rose Coser found in her study of the staff of a mental hospital that there was a consistent pattern in the direction of humorous remarks—the jokes flowed down. High-status people initiated more jokes and witty remarks than low-status workers. The amount of joking decreased down the hierarchy: Of 90 witticisms, 53 were by senior staff members, 33 by junior staff members, and only 4 by the paramedical staff, who made up at least one-third of the group.

"Humor and wit always contain some aggression," writes Coser, "whether or not it is directed against a manifest target." But frequently there is a direct target. In her study, 86 of 100 witticisms were directed at someone, such as a staff member, a patient, or the self. The most frequent target of the senior staff was junior staff members; for junior staff, it was patients and patients' relatives. The paramedical staff, in the few witticisms they initiated, directed jokes toward patients or themselves. In other words, humor tended to be directed against those who had no authority over the humorist. In more than twenty meetings over a three-month period, only twice did a junior staff member make a joke about a senior staffer—and never about one who was present. Coser concluded from her study that humor in work situations is used not only to resolve social conflicts, but to support the social structure.

Although women would do well to learn to use humor at work, Coser's research—and common sense—tell us that in the presence of superiors, they must test the waters carefully. One explanation Coser offers for junior staff members in her study using humor less is that it may be interpreted as a challenge to the senior staffers who are in control of the meeting. Humor, for the junior members, is a risky tool, because through aggression it takes control temporarily out of the hands of those higher up. "The *diversion* that humor affords," says Coser, "may also have the latent function of *subversion*."

The study also offers an explanation for why women are often the targets of humor: They are likely to be at the lower ends of a job hierarchy. There's something else going on, however, something more fundamental that may cause serious problems for working women: *Both* sexes find it funnier when a woman is the butt of a joke.

When Women Are Put Down, Everyone Laughs

That's what communications professors Joanne Cantor, of the University of Wisconsin, and Indiana University's Dolf Zillmann found in two studies conducted in the seventies. In the first study, involving 34 male and 34 female college students, half the subjects were given booklets with jokes showing men dominating or having the last laugh over women; the other half were given jokes showing women coming out on top.

The jokes were like the following, an example of a male-dominates-female joke:

"A movie actor, soon after his autobiography was published, was approached at a party by an actress, who said, 'I saw your new book . . . Who wrote it for you?'

" 'I'm so glad you enjoyed it,' came the reply. 'Who read it to you?' "

Both female and male subjects found this version of the joke significantly funnier than the same joke with the sexes reversed, so that the man was ridiculed by the woman.

Not satisfied with the outcome, Joanne Cantor replicated it several years later—and got the same results. Women and men still found it funnier when the woman was the butt of the joke.

Given this research, it is little wonder that some women are accused of lacking a sense of humor. Maybe they just don't find funny what most people do: Seeing a woman put down.

Plenty of women have learned—consciously or not—that an easy way to get a laugh is to deride a woman. And often the most convenient target is the joke-teller herself. Self-ridicule is characteristic of much humor used by women; in fact, it may be one of the most significant differences in humor between men and women.

The popular notion is that those who can poke fun at themselves are well adjusted and have a good sense of humor. People continually make light of their shortcomings, mistakes, and humiliations. Konrad Lorenz writes, "We are all radically intolerant of pompous or sanctimonious people, because we expect a certain amount of self-ridicule in every intelligent human being."

Self-disparagement can help us rise above feelings of inferiority —if we mock our weaknesses we separate ourselves from them. Whatever soothing effect such humor may have on the psyche, however, and despite the popular notions telling us about the value of self-deprecating humor in winning friends, there's strong evidence that it is a tactic women—especially in the company of powerful men—would do well without.

Studies show that men and women have very different views of self-administered put-downs. Professor Zillmann and S. Holly Stocking, then a doctoral student at Indiana University, tested whether people do, in fact, enjoy seeing others put themselves down. They also wanted to find out what people think of those who use self-deprecating humor. Do we truly admire them and applaud their ability not to take themselves too seriously?

The results showed a clear-cut and surprising sex difference: Women find self-deprecating humor altogether funnier than men do; males dislike such humor no matter who is doing it.

Women not only find this kind of humor funnier than men do, they like the people who put themselves down better. In their studies, Zillmann and Stocking asked the subjects to rate the jokers on specific personal characteristics. Men consistently rated the self-deprecators as significantly less confident, intelligent, and witty than one who disparaged a friend or enemy. But women consistently showed a more favorable attitude toward the self-disparager, male or female, than men did.

The difference in the way the sexes view self-ridicule may lie, as Zillmann and Stocking suggest, in the way each sex views dominance. Men typically strive for dominance as part of their sex identity, whereas females more readily accept domination. "Because of its apparently negative consequences for 'machismo,' self-disparagement holds little promise for the male. Even when presented in a humorous fashion, it gives little cause to rejoice, for the blow to the male ego may be too serious a matter to warrant laughter."

When humor needs a target, men usually prefer trying to better one another by trading put-downs; there is no challenge for them in self-deprecating humor. One reason women use this kind of humor may be that they have, or think they have, fewer targets. If they want to get a laugh, the easiest way is to ridicule themselves. For working women especially, however, the price of that laughter may be too high. Self-ridicule may merely reinforce a woman's bottom-rung position.

Some women may use self-deprecating humor as a way of not being overly threatening to men. If a women turns a little joke on herself, then the men can say, "Oh, okay, she's not really pushy." Such behavior is useful, of course, only if a woman *wants* to appear nonthreatening. And on the job, that may seldom be the case. If you want to get ahead, there's not much to be gained in drawing attention to your weaknesses, through humor or otherwise. If you make much of your shortcomings, they will soon be obvious to everyone. A woman, for example, who makes a repeated joke about her inability to file her sales reports on schedule, because her field representatives are routinely tardy, may for the moment diffuse the tension, but she won't gain the respect of women or men. And she's admitting that she's not fulfilling her duties.

Self-deprecation used with subordinates is no more effective. One male boss who supervised a group of high-tech engineers had a way of ducking behind such humor whenever discussions with his engineers moved into topics he wasn't knowledgeable about. He would say, "Well, that's why we hired you. You're more clever than I am when it comes to this." One man who worked for him said that although he thought his boss was saying, "This is difficult work and you guys are doing a good job," he still found the remark disingenuous and condescending. A woman would fare no better using that kind of humor in the same situation.

In some circumstances, of course, high-status people can and do effectively make jokes on themselves, particularly when they want to deflect criticism. When a mistake or deficiency can't be ignored, pointing it out yourself denies others the opportunity to do so and, in the end, often serves to save face. But as a rule, anyone, regardless of sex, who wants to be viewed as a leader and to dominate others will not use self-ridicule.

GETTING IN ON THE JOKE

Although working women would do well to abandon frequent use of self-ridicule, and to make judicious use of hostile humor directed at superiors, they shouldn't conclude that humor doesn't belong on the job. Effective use of humor to ease relationships and build camaraderie with men can be an important tool for making men comfortable. It also can put a woman in control; humor helps define and distinguish the leaders of a group. Too often, however, women retreat behind a serious demeanor.

One man in his late twenties, Martin, remembered the sharply different experiences he had interviewing for a summer internship several years ago. One interview was conducted by a woman who played the whole thing straight and made him very uneasy. "She actually asked me to name ten weaknesses and ten strengths," he says. "I was twenty years old. If I *had* ten of each, I sure didn't know what they were." For another summer position he was questioned by two men. They started the interview by asking him where he was from. The conversation went like this:

"Chicago."

"Oh, yeah? Where?"

"Well, not actually Chicago, but nearby."

"Oh, yeah? Where?"

"Well, a little town southeast of Chicago."

"Oh, yeah? Where?"

By that time all three were laughing. Remembering the situation, Martin laughs now and says, "Yeah, they gave me a lot of trash."

It's that sort of "trash"—the give-and-take banter men enjoy—that women can use just as effectively. In fact, one of the most important tactics a woman must learn in order to use humor well with men is to participate in that type of humor. She must learn to return jokes and barbs, rather than collapse when a man shoots one her way. Complaining about the women in his new office, a man said that one woman in particular took everything too seriously. "She never has any fun," he says. "I just can't joke with her."

Getting in on the joke often means taking lightly men's jokes—or at least making them think you're taking them lightly. One woman arrived at work Monday morning with her left arm heavily wrapped in gauze. She had slipped on a ladder while trying to put up screens on her house and had ripped open her wrist; the rest of her Sunday afternoon had been spent in a hospital emergency room getting stitched up. When she passed a group of male colleagues on her way into her office, one said, "Hey, what happened to you? Tried to commit suicide?" Rather than taking offense at the tactless comment or offering a serious explanation, she got a laugh and scored a few points by throwing back a remark of her own: "Yes, it was the thought of facing Monday with you guys that made me do it."

Women may be the targets of a man's jokes for a number of reasons. It may very well be that the man feels hostile toward women and enjoys releasing tension and aggression in direct—but safe—attacks. Even if you suspect that's the reason, the best response is still to show you can participate in the give-and-take. It's futile to confront the joker; a serious response only brings further ridicule—"What's the matter? Can't you take a joke?"

Although initiating humor is more strongly associated with males than females, it is a less obvious intrusion into traditional masculinity than more direct expressions of dominance and aggression. And it is a tactic women can and should try more often. Handling humor effectively, in fact, may be one of the most important on-the-job skills a woman needs. "That's because humor can help to diffuse tense situations," says a female vice president, "and women get into plenty of those."

5 WHAT MEN VALUE MOST

Consider this: There's a fellow named Heinz whose wife is dying. A pharmacist has a drug that could save her, but Heinz doesn't have enough money to pay for it and the druggist isn't offering any discounts. Should Heinz steal the drug?

Some people see that as a fairly straightforward question with a straightforward answer: "Yes." They see a conflict between property and life, and select life as having the higher value.

Others view the question differently. "That's tough," they say. Or, "There must be some other way. Couldn't Heinz talk it out with the druggist?" Or, "There's surely some way to come up with the money. What would happen to Heinz's wife if he were arrested for stealing the drug?" These people see more to the question; they take into account the ramifications of the choices to be made.

The alternative ways of considering Heinz's dilemma are representative of two ways of thinking and of solving moral problems. The first is based on justice: What's the *right* action here? Those who think that way focus on clear-cut principles—in this instance, life is more valuable than property—and let that determine their decision. The second group is more concerned with caring: What is the *responsible* action to take? These people want to know the particulars of the situation, and they think about the relationships involved. They look beyond the immediate question to consider what will happen over time.

And there's something else about these two ways of thinking: Men are more likely to follow the first pattern, women the second.

Carol Gilligan, a psychologist at the Harvard Graduate School of

Education, spent more than a decade in research on moral development and made that startling discovery: Men and women differ in their values and how they perceive morality. For women, the most cherished value is *caring*, for men it is *justice*. Those different orientations affect how men and women think, what they fear, how they connect with others, and what their strengths are.

MEN ARE THE STANDARD

For centuries, Gilligan contends, society has listened to the voices of men and has based its theories of moral and psychological development on their experiences. The male way of thinking has been seen by psychologists not as *one* way of thinking, but as the *best* way. Over a period of twenty years, Harvard psychologist Lawrence Kohlberg developed a theory of moral development that was widely accepted until recently challenged by Gilligan and others. Kohlberg's theory describes six stages of moral development that form a hierarchy, a series of moral stages that individuals pass through one step at a time as they mature. At the highest level, a person's thinking is governed by the moral principles that underlie society. Of course, not everyone reaches the highest level on the Kohlberg scale, only those who are fully developed morally. Criminals and children test near the bottom of the scale. And, oh yes, women. They generally get stuck somewhere in the middle.

On Kohlberg's scale, women seldom progress past stage three, which is where the Golden Rule and the need to be a good person guide. At this level a person holds "right" to be living up to what others expect of you, having good motives, showing concern for others, and upholding mutual relationships, such as trust and loyalty, respect and gratitude. A more advanced person, according to Kohlberg's theory, moves beyond such considerations to an understanding of the moral principles that support society, and is guided by them even when they conflict with social rules.

When Gilligan noticed that women rarely advanced to the top

levels, she didn't ask what was wrong with women, she wondered what was wrong with the scale. What was amiss was that Kohlberg had failed to consider women in his studies; he had tested only men—using problems like the Heinz dilemma—and had developed his theory on their responses, claiming universality.

Gilligan conducted her own studies on both men and women and discovered two patterns of moral thought. In her book *In a Different Voice*, which reports the results of her efforts to find how men and women resolve moral conflict and how they define themselves morally, she calls for a recognition of the two types of social experience. We would all benefit, she argues, from an expanded theory of moral development that included the feminine voice. Not too much to ask, really.

The contrasts between the two ways of thinking can be seen clearly in the voices Kohlberg and Gilligan report. Kohlberg cites the responses of Joe, a twenty-four-year-old man in his study, as an example of the top-level thinking and decision making. The peculiarities of any given situation do not concern Joe; he is guided by principles. When asked what morality and moral right meant to him, Joe said, "Recognizing the rights of other individuals, first to life and then to do as he pleases as long as it doesn't interfere with somebody else's rights."

Joe's detachment and formality differ sharply from the voices of women in Gilligan's book, who describe what morality means to them. One says: "When I think of the word *morality*, I think of obligations. I usually think of it as conflicts between personal desires and . . . social considerations . . . A truly moral person would always consider another person as their equal." Another says, "I relate morality with interpersonal relationships that have to do with respect for the other person and myself."

Gilligan found a moral conception different from the one Joe illustrates. It is a morality that arises from conflicting *responsibilities*, rather than conflicting *rights*, and that uses a way of thinking that is contextual and narrative, rather than abstract, for the resolution of problems. Judging women by men's standards, as Kohlberg has, not only wrongly places women below men in the moral hierarchy, but ignores a significant body of moral thought.

HOW MORAL DECISIONS ARE MADE

Women's decisions tend to be guided by the circumstances of a situation; they consider various possibilities and contingencies. They consider how one choice precludes others. Men tend to think in a more linear, one-dimensional way; they are less likely to look at externalities. A problem for a woman, therefore, can have greater ambiguity and complexity than it would for a man. As a result, women sometimes must exercise caution to avoid being misunderstood by men. Depending on how you handle yourself, expressing the ambiguity you see in a problem could make you appear doubtful and confused, a victim of divided judgment, or it could indicate the depth of your thought and your far-ranging, analytical perceptions of the implications of a problem.

Although men and women are not likely to be making life-and-death moral decisions in their daily work, their divergent decision-making patterns influence all their thinking. At work, they may take separate paths to a decision, though they won't necessarily arrive at disparate answers. Sometimes, however, different paths will lead to different conclusions.

JoAnn, a woman who works for a large corporation in a service industry, found herself in serious trouble because the decisions she made differed from her superior's expectations. As a manager in the customer relations department, she was responsible for billing and overseeing orders placed by corporate customers.

The corporation's relationships with its customers were governed by complex contractual agreements that were subject to state laws and regulations, which had been hammered out over many years. JoAnn ran into trouble when she failed to rely on those contracts and instead responded to individual situations. When clients called

JoAnn with questions and suggestions for how they should be billed in some new circumstance, she often would strike new agreements with them. JoAnn's ability to perceive the client's viewpoint, and the many factors making each situation unique, led her to reach decisions based on those insights—to her company's detriment. Although the customer's arguments for why billing should be handled in a particular way were often reasonable, the contingencies in each individual situation were, in fact, irrelevant. The contract spelled out clearly how billing should be done.

JoAnn's superiors were confused and angered by her behavior, and she was in danger of losing her job. One of her male colleagues said, "I don't know what her problem is. She's smart, but she keeps screwing up." And she was equally confused by her own failure to understand where she was going wrong. Was she thinking in a way different from the men who expected her to follow the rules? Was she failing to make decisions in the "male" way—to find a principle and apply it to the problem? Or did she simply fail to understand the role she should have been playing in her job? It's impossible to say just what was going on, but perhaps if she had been aware of the possibility that her decision-making paths were different from those of the men around her, she might have saved herself from making serious errors.

THE RELATIONSHIP FACTOR

For many women, simply recognizing that they have different ways of thinking from men is a significant and enlightening step. Few women have failed to suspect the truth of that, and yet knowing it is so can help women respect their own thinking and help them resist adopting a masculine style that may not fit. Furthermore, both these ways of thinking and decision making have their strengths and uses in the workplace. One style does not necessarily preclude the other. And a woman doesn't have to "think like a man" to understand male thinking.

If a woman can carry into the workplace what she knows about the different patterns of thinking she'll be at an advantage—better able to understand how she arrived at her decisions and better able to understand what's going on in the minds of men around her.

The high value women place on caring can lead them to include concern for interpersonal relationships when confronted with an issue or problem. Men, who are more externally oriented toward a project or goal, tend not to weigh the effects of alternative solutions on relationships. Washington, D.C.–based management consultant Denise Cavanaugh explains the distinction this way: "For men, relationships are often a means to an end, for women they are often an end in themselves." Both perceptions lend something valuable to on-the-job decisions.

For example, two members of a hospital strategic planning committee, a man and a woman, saw a problem from different vantage points. The committee was developing for the hospital a new division for home health care, a need they saw as increasing over time and as vital to the future profitability of the hospital. A woman on the committee immediately saw the importance of how the nursing staff would see this new division. Part of its success would depend on the enthusiasm of the nurses who would provide the home care, and yet this woman knew that nurses view home care as less challenging than acute care. She realized that when the new division was announced, it would be important to present a transfer into the division as a promotion, as an opportunity to be on the leading edge of the hospital's activities. "What will the nurses think?" was high on her list of concerns about how well the new project would work.

A man on the committee was not blind to the people problems, but he saw them differently. He stressed the importance of getting a good team of people together who could get the job done. He was not keyed into what the individual nurses would think about how this move would affect their careers or how well they would like the work. Combining his perceptions with the woman's appeared a good formula for developing a successful approach for the project.

Recognizing that your values and the way you arrive at decisions may differ from those of the men you work with can also help you understand why your emotions may be in turmoil in a situation where a man's would be more detached. Perceiving the human impact of decisions is part of a valuable perspective that women can bring to work. That human understanding gives women a sensitivity to co-workers, clients, customers, and competitors that men sometimes lack. At times, however, that interpersonal perspective can make it difficult for women to carry out business decisions.

A woman who owns a business says that one of her difficulties as a boss was learning to fire employees. That's not a pleasant task for any manager, of course, but for her it was more than unpleasant, it conflicted with her sense of herself. "The first time I had to fire someone," she says, "it absolutely went against everything I was taught as a woman. It was such an offensive thing. No matter how liberal our upbringing, we're taught not to make waves. We're told: 'Yes, you can be successful, but don't rock the boat while you're trying. And do try to make a nice warm atmosphere around you.' "

The second firing was easier for her. Although she was still troubled by the impact her decision had on the lives of others, her earlier experience helped her to accept more easily the correctness of her decision for her business and herself. Contrast that with the seeming ease with which one man accepted being promoted over a good friend, who then quit because he couldn't bear the situation: "It's too bad it interfered with our friendship, but this is business." Adhering to a rule—keep business separate from personal concerns—permitted him to accept the situation with apparent ease.

Both people made correct assessments: The man recognized he couldn't do anything about his friend's problem (certainly not refuse a job he wanted and deserved), and the woman recognized that despite the emotional discomfort her decision caused her and others, her decision was correct. The problem for women comes when they expect themselves to behave like and share the emotions of men, berating themselves for not being able to maintain the detachment and the adherence to rules that often enables men to face the human implications of business decisions with equanimity.

PLAYING BY THE RULES

The differing values of men and women show up in their attitudes toward rules, which are more important to males and play a greater role in their decision making. Psychologists have long observed that boys are fascinated with elaborate rules and procedures for fair play, whereas girls are more tolerant toward exceptions and innovations in the rules. Girls are likely to adjust the rules as they go along to suit the skills and desires of individual players. In a game of softball, for instance, a group of girls might let one who was a poor batter take extra swings at the ball, or they might replay a ball if it wasn't clear whether it landed in or out of bounds.

Boys would be unlikely to bend the "three strikes you're out" and "on-the-line is in-bounds" rules; they take great care in establishing rules and pride themselves in sticking to them. They want to win and play well within the limits of the game. If the rules are bent for one boy, he then doesn't know how to measure himself against the others. To girls, the rules are less important than their relationships with one another.

Keeping Cool

The reigning value and one of the most important unwritten rules of male behavior on the playing field and in the office is keeping a cool façade.

In studies of sex differences, researchers have tried to determine whether females are more timid than males, as popular thinking would have it. The only distinction that turns up, however, is that females are more willing to admit to feeling timid or anxious than males are. Boys, for example, when asked whether they sometimes dream about things they don't like to talk about or whether they feel bad when one of their friends won't play with them, are likely to say no. Such denial is generally interpreted as defensiveness, since those situations are thought to be universal and to provoke anxiety. Boys also rate higher on defensiveness scales that measure how much someone disguises his true evaluation of himself in an attempt to present a wholly favorable impression.

Presenting and maintaining that favorable front and revealing no emotion is extremely important to men at work. Men value their calculated and deductive decision-making processes. They expect themselves and their colleagues to behave in unemotional, logical ways. One man tells of being in a large meeting where one participant, Sam, was at the center of the discussion. Question after question was directed to him. Although the questions were not hostile, Sam knew it was important to perform well, to respond thoroughly and carefully, and to explain the issues under discussion, which were in his area of responsibility. Each question increased the pressure Sam felt; and as he talked he fiddled with a ballpoint pen. Suddenly there was a sharp snap heard around the table; Sam had gripped the pen so hard he had broken it. He and everyone else ignored the incident; Sam continued talking without pause as ink ran down his hand and shirtsleeve.

The man who observed this told the story later in a mixed-sex group. The women present were impressed by Sam's ability to carry on in a tense situation after the embarrassment of making a mess with the pen. One woman asked the storyteller whether he too admired his co-worker's control. "No," he said, "because Sam should never have shown how up-tight he was in the first place; he didn't have the 'right stuff.' " By breaking the keep-cool code, Sam made everyone at the meeting uncomfortable, and, more important, having lost prestige with the other participants, his views were discounted.

The women who heard this story missed the point. They understood the keep-cool maxim, but not the underlying principle. The male code is not that men should *hide* emotion; it is that they should not have it at all. Failing that, a man should never, as Sam did, let the emotion surface, thereby revealing that he has lost his detachment, his ability to behave in a dispassionate, deductive manner.

Successful, powerful women learn to adhere to this code. Dorothy Gregg of Research & Forecasts was the first woman vice president at Celanese Corporation. She learned quickly that, especially at the upper ranks, understatement reigns; no extreme emotions, no displays of feeling are allowed.

"At the first meeting of senior officers that I attended at Celanese," she says, "I thought they were all puppets seated around the table. There wasn't a human expression in that room. And when I spontaneously said something, they were all shocked. It was like a poker game where everyone kept a façade." When she spoke up, there was a tremor around the room, then an embarrassed silence. When it became clear that she wasn't going to carry on and that her misstep was evident to her, the men settled back. "After that," Dorothy says, "everyone expects you to behave if you have any sense at all. Otherwise you're moved to a padded cell."

Emotional control is important to men for several reasons. One is that, as one man says, "you show your hand" if you permit colleagues or competitors to see how you feel about something. Another is that men are generally uncomfortable with emotional displays; business relationships are easier for them if everyone behaves with a certain amount of detachment. Men tend not to place a high value on candidness and emotion—in fact, they consider such traits to be weaknesses. Stoicism is characteristic of successful people. As a male mentor put it to one woman, "Big guys don't shake."

MEN LOATHE WOMEN'S TEARS

Emotional displays in a business setting are offensive to men because of the high value they place on control. Crying is the ultimate transgression and can cost a woman a lot. One reason men dislike seeing a woman cry is that they don't understand women's tears. "Where do they come from?" asks one man. Men don't understand that women cry for any number of reasons: to relieve tension, anxiety, and frustration, for instance. Just because a woman cries doesn't mean she's deeply sad or in intense pain. But few men understand that. They don't realize that a woman can be only mildly upset and still feel the need for tears.

A woman who teaches management education seminars says that the men she encounters assume that when a woman cries she is in the same emotional state a man would be in if he were in tears. And a man seldom cries, as she says, "until he's ready for the rubber room."

Men learn to associate tears with weakness. As boys, they grow up being taught not to cry. They learn to keep a stiff upper lip no matter what happens or how much things hurt. They learn that if they're going to play in the big boys' games, they have to act the way big boys act. And big boys *don't* cry.

The main reason a woman's tears are upsetting to men, however, is that men have been taught to feel guilty over a woman's tears—and to distrust them. It is a rare man who, as a man or a boy, has not been manipulated by a female's tears—and it is a rare female who has not at some time in her life used tears as a weapon. Tears are the traditional control mechanism of the powerless—women and children. What little sister doesn't learn that pitiful tears at the right moment will get her brother off her back? All it takes is one such experience, especially if little sister delivers a smirk once she gets her way, to teach a little boy not to trust female tears. Guilt joins distrust when he hears from Mom—or worse, Dad—"Now look what you've done! You've made her cry." Unfortunately, no small number of *grown* women also use tears as a convenient method of controlling recalcitrant males. Men associate tears with their personal lives, with guilt, and with fear. Those are good reasons for a woman to avoid crying in front of men in work situations. In addition, it's helpful to remember that, for the most part, women must play by men's rules at work; it's their game. Men have their emotions in control, and so must women.

Crying not only causes women to lose power, but it costs them in another way. Some men are so fearful of provoking tears that they avoid criticizing women's work and leave them out of difficult situations. Madelyn Jennings, a vice president at Gannett Company, says, "If you want to put a man under the table—cry. Nothing makes a man more upset or nervous than a woman crying."

She remembers a time when something she had been in charge of bombed and she was called on the carpet by two male superiors. Later the word got back to her that both had said they were relieved that she hadn't cried when her failure was discussed. The men had dreaded the meeting, fearing it would provoke tears. As healthy and normal as crying may be, in the business world criers are second class. Jennings knew that and was determined not to handicap herself. Throughout the meeting she repeated to herself "like a mantra, 'I will *not*.' " She succeeded and the victory was important to her future success.

Another woman, Rachel, learned the hard way that tears in business meetings do more harm than good. As an outreach counselor for a school district, her job was to circulate to various schools throughout a wide area and help teachers develop new programs. She didn't get along well with her male boss and suspected that was due at least in part to his discomfort with the freedom and independence her job provided. He saw her as being out of his control because she wasn't required to be in the office. He checked up on her frequently, calling schools to make sure she was doing her rounds. He became increasingly unhappy with her and finally wrongly accused her of using work time for personal business. Rachel confronted him, to "clear the air," because she couldn't bear being doubted and knew her denials hadn't penetrated. She became so upset during the meeting when he refused to believe her that she cried. The tears helped temporarily. "He softened," she says, "but it put him on top." Rachel disliked him even more for, as she says, "putting me in a situation that made me cry." She didn't like her own behavior or his, and the incident irreparably damaged their relationship. She eventually quit the job.

When a woman cries in front of a man at work, she tells him that she doesn't have the "right stuff" and isn't willing to play the game according to the rules. In the short run, she may get her way or may even get out of a tough situation, but in the long run she'll lose heavily because the man will no longer see her as a potential contender for the big stakes; she will have shown she can't be trusted not to tip her hand to an opponent or to keep her emotions under control.

TEAM PLAY

The experience men get as children playing team sports is often given credit for the greater success men seem to have at work. Although working women frequently refer to the theory as a cliché, many nonetheless suspect it is accurate. Men do seem to be more effective team players; and it would appear that their almost universal boyhood experience with team sports accounts for that success. But that's not the only factor.

What we know about the psychology of women and their values systems tells us women should be champion team players—and in a sense they are. Women tend to be cooperative, egalitarian, sensitive to the needs of individuals within the group, and perceptive about behaving in a way that is responsible toward others. Those are important qualities for a team player. Those same characteristics, however, also can contribute to what women lack in team play. Although women generally work well cooperatively, they seem less able to cooperate with people they don't like and lack the ability to *seem* to like them. Says one young woman who is struggling to fit in with the powerful men at her workplace, "I think team sports teach you that there are a lot of jerks in powerful positions who you have to listen to and find some way of accomplishing your goals within theirs. You are an individual but have to work with the group." A female who grew up with sisters, she laments that she had little experience as a child playing team games.

A woman doesn't need to spend time on a baseball diamond or basketball court, however, in order to learn the essentials of team play. All women need to learn and practice is a simple lesson men have mastered: *You don't have to like the people you work with.* Although the impulse of women to build relationships and break down barriers between themselves and others is strong—and valuable—once a woman understands she doesn't have to do that at work she's on her way to being a more effective team player.

It seems paradoxical, but because relationships tend not to be as important to men as they are to women, it is easier for men to build relationships at work. They can more easily develop camaraderie with people they don't like. Men engage in backslapping, joking, and banter with men they may feel nothing for or may even dislike. The methods women use to express and build goodwill—hugging, sharing possessions, trading intimate details about themselves—are most likely done only with other women they care for.

As women gain experience working with men, they learn that business is not necessarily conducted among friends. Says Dorothy Gregg, "Everything in business is based on reciprocity. 'You can do something for me, I can do something for you.' Men understand this perfectly." And they understand they don't have to be friends to work together. "They can loathe each other," says Gregg. "I've been in a room many times when men have reached some kind of deal that seems to you to be perfectly amiable; they're joking together and they seem to be good friends, but when one walks out the door the CEO will say, 'He's the world's greatest ass. I loathe him.' You say to yourself, 'What superb playacting,' and it *is* acting."

Women, too, can be very good at acting. The problem for them, however, is that they tend to see themselves as being disingenuous or hypocritical when they do it. Men, who more easily see relationships as a means to an end, are less likely to suffer that conflict. If a woman is carrying around an inner message that says relationships are always an end in themselves, then she'll have trouble playacting when it is useful to do so in business. Women need to remember that they, too, often have "means to an end" relationships that are more expedient than honest. We all get along with certain people in our lives (such as some relatives) for the sake of convenience—and that's okay. And it's okay to engage in those relationships at work too. A little guile can be useful on the job.

GETTING BY WITHOUT COMPLIMENTS

The detachment that men maintain in their work relationships also makes it easier for them to accept criticism, and, sometimes, to go without compliments and encouragement. It's foolish to think that men don't enjoy—and often need—support and encouragement, just as women do. Many a manager, male and female, has learned the power of praise in getting subordinates to perform. Nonetheless, women seem to suffer more from the lack of praise and seem to take slights to heart in a way men don't. Male colleagues and bosses are often more closed and less forthcoming than women would like them to be.

The code of the business world, as established by men, is: Nothing said means all is well. A woman who has had a lot of experience working in male environments says she has learned to assume things are going well when she hears nothing about her performance. "When things have gone badly, I do get some feedback," she says. She has worked with men so much, in fact, that when she's around women, who tend to be quick with positive response, she becomes confused and a bit suspicious, just as a man might be.

Women must learn to accept that in the corporate culture blame, not praise, is the norm. You're expected to do a good job; if you do an outstanding one, then it shows up in your bonus and paycheck. One woman, now a vice president of a large company, says she started out her career wanting and seeking approval, but learned—slowly and painfully—to let go of that A-student mentality. "If you go into the corporate world desperately needing approval, it's going to inhibit you as an executive because there's just not a lot of head-patting there. You'll be pursuing something that doesn't exist and you'll leave yourself emotionally vulnerable. But more important, God help you if you are fool enough to settle for a pat on the head. Raises and promotions are what really count. Approval is cheap."

6 THE PSYCHOLOGY OF MEN

The study of human psychology has largely been a study of male psychology. The psyche of the male, child and adult, has been measured, probed, and plotted, and on the patterns discovered, theories about human development have been drawn. When women are measured against those theories, they are not a perfect fit. In the world of psychological paradigms and psychoanalytic theory, the development of males is straightforward and logical; boys fit the rules. Girls present theoretical puzzles. Where females differ from the male/human model, they often have been labeled deviant or inadequate.

Most notable among the important male-based psychological theories are those of Sigmund Freud, who admitted confusion about women, referring to female sex identity as "a dark continent for psychology." Acknowledging that he had used the male child to develop his theories, he wrote, "With little girls, so we have supposed, things must be similar, though in some way or other they must nevertheless be different."

Freud's theories assumed a male norm and determined how women differed; accordingly, females were depicted as castrated males who longed for what they lacked. Psychoanalyst Karen Horney challenged Freud's theory of penis envy and pointed out that psychoanalysis was a male-dominated field. Writing in the 1920s, she said that "till recently the minds of boys and men only were taken as objects of investigation. The reason for this is obvious. Psychoanalysis is the creation of a male genius, and almost all those who have developed his ideas have been men. It is only right and reasonable that they should evolve more easily a masculine psychology and understand more the development of men than of women."

The protestations of Horney and other psychoanalysts of the time stimulated much debate, but didn't deter others who followed from continuing to study males and build upon male theoretical models. Today that's beginning to change.

A number of researchers, among them Carol Gilligan, Carol Jacklin, Grace Baruch, and Rosalind Barnett, are currently working to redefine human nature by including the perspectives and experiences of women. And Jean Baker Miller, in *Toward a New Psychology of Women*, published in 1976, called for a recognition of the truths of feminine experience in the development of theories of human nature. She writes: "Since man is the measure of all things—and man, literally, rather than human beings—we have all tended to measure ourselves by men. Men's interpretations of the world defines and directs us all, tells us what is the nature of human nature."

Recognizing differences in female and male psychological traits can be valuable to working women. In order to work effectively with men you need to learn what makes men tick and use that knowledge to your advantage on the job. Your knowledge of sex differences in psychological development also can help you use some feminine characteristics to your advantage, while acknowledging that in a work world dominated by men some traits must be de-emphasized if you are to succeed. Understanding psychological sex differences and how we come to be the way we are begins, as you might guess, with mother.

THE ROLE OF MOTHER

A critical difference in the ways males and females develop, the one on which all other distinctions may hang, is the issue of separation. Traditional human development theories assume that maturing depends on separating; as children we are dependent upon and deeply attached to others; as adults we are expected to be independent. Carol Gilligan found in her studies that women remain closely tied to other people even as adults. To Freud and other theorists who based their ideas on the male child, a woman's failure to separate amounts to a failure in her development. To Gilligan, it is not an aberration, but rather a sign that women are in touch with the reality that we are all connected and interdependent.

Gilligan suggests that the important differences between male and female come from the disparate experiences that each has in the care they get from mother and from their responses to their early attachment to her. It is there that the sexes develop their different views of separation and attachment. Girls find their identity from seeing themselves as being *like* mother and boys from being *not like* mother. Thus for males it is critical to their development of self that they separate from their mothers; for women and girls separation is not necessary. The result, according to Gilligan, is that masculinity is defined through separation, femininity through attachment. Each sex is threatened by the opposite force. Males are threatened by intimacy and have difficulty developing relationships with others, while females are threatened by separation and have difficulty establishing their identities outside personal relationships.

Other psychologists have argued that the male need to separate gives men a less secure gender identity. Before a male learns what he can be, he has to face what he can't be—that is, female like mother. His search for a sexual identity, then, is a negative one— he knows more what he is not than what he is.

In order for little boys to find themselves, they deny their attachment to mother and repress anything in themselves that is feminine; some theorists contend that they also come to denigrate all that is feminine in their effort to be masculine. The struggle is not something that is settled in boyhood; it carries on throughout a man's entire life. In *The Seasons of a Man's Life,* a report of his study of forty men at midlife, Yale psychologist Daniel Levinson writes that young men starting out in the adult world and trying to live up to the images of masculinity tend to neglect the feminine aspects of themselves. "Any part of the self that he regards as feminine is experienced as dangerous," Levinson writes. "A young man struggling to sustain his manliness is frightened by feelings and interests that seem womanly.''

For many men the danger in all things feminine remains a powerful force in their lives. For a man to be a man he must be different from women. Boys and men go to lengths females would never consider to distinguish themselves from the opposite sex. In the simplest example, girls and women have long worn men's clothing without risking loss of femininity, but for a man to wear women's clothing is to signal sexual deviance. Women can and do take on any number of masculine traits and roles—such as working in jobs traditionally occupied by men—without threat to their sexual identities. Men, however, are much more fearful of doing anything that seems feminine or of seeming feminine in their emotions or outlook. Their sexual identity is more tenuous and needs continual reinforcement. That need leads to much of the male gang behavior that serves to separate them from women. More on that behavior, and how to cope with it, can be found later in this chapter, and in the chapters on language, humor, making men comfortable, and competition.

Some psychologists and, in particular, psychoanalysts say the close mother-child tie is responsible not only for the tenuousness of the masculine identity and fear of appearing feminine, but also for what many theorists—those at odds with Freud—contend is a male fear of dependency on women. They maintain that men fear the consequences of dependency on women, which to men means the loss of masculinity, so much that they segregate and dominate women. Karen Horney linked men's fear of women to the boy's fear of loss of self-esteem that would come if he were rebuffed by mother. Horney saw that fear as the primary motivation in men's compulsion to prove their manhood. Others argue that social institutions, even the most primitive, are designed to defend men against their fears of women by containing women and controlling their behavior.

Although most men keep their fear of women and emasculation fairly well in check, not all do, which can cause problems at work. One way the fear is likely to be exhibited is in men feeling threatened by women who show signs of dominance. And that, obviously, puts women in a difficult position. A working woman cannot avoid dominant, powerful behavior unless she is content to be subordinate to men, and yet if she exerts power, she risks threatening men. What a women must learn is to be aggressive and dominant in the right places and at the right times. Working women have been told to be aggressive so often in the past few years that some have gone overboard—out-aggressing the men and being unable to ask for a paper clip without employing intimidation tactics. Controlled and managed aggression is the key. A woman, for example, may wish to impress superiors with her ability to assume the take-charge role with her subordinates or to be aggressive with clients, but she must be careful not to direct those traits at bosses.

Not only are men afraid of being dominated by women and of appearing to be feminine, they are, according to some theorists, paradoxically envious of women's unique characteristics. Horney, and later Margaret Mead, argued that men envy and even regard women with awe because of their capacity for motherhood. Horney suggested that both sexes initially see the superiority of women's wombs, with their capacity to create a child, over the male genitalia. She said she saw in her male patients an intense envy of pregnancy, childbirth, and suckling.

Whether you accept the notion of womb envy any more than that of penis envy, simple logic tells us that the different anatomies of the sexes must lead to somewhat different development of the sexes. Use your knowledge of male psychology to supplement your understanding of men in general and to help you understand how you are different. The more you understand sex differences, the less you'll be tempted to blame yourself or assume you're wrong when you respond differently from men. And you'll be in a better position to manage your own behavior.

ATTACHMENT AND SEPARATION

One area of psychology that working women particularly need to understand is the different orientations of men and women toward

intimacy and separation. It can affect how the sexes behave at
work—and it can occasionally put women at odds with men.

Men create distances between themselves and others by asserting
status and dominance. Women, by minimizing status and stressing
affiliation and equality, draw others closer to them. And that can
lead to on-the-job conflicts between men and women. One woman,
a specialist in using music and theater with children, was conducting
a seminar in her methods for a group of elementary school teachers.
It was her first such experience, and she was being observed by her
male boss from the learning center where she was employed. She
began the class by telling the students she was nervous. She attempted
to diffuse her tension by using a "we're all in this together" approach, minimizing the distance between herself and her students,
which made her uncomfortable. Later, her boss reprimanded her for
taking that stance; he felt strongly that she should have built upon
her authority and kept herself distinct from—and above—her students. He considered her admission of nervousness to be a serious
mistake. Like most males, he preferred to establish a pecking order;
the woman, like most females, was more comfortable creating a
horizontal pattern of relationships, "links rather than ladders," as
one researcher describes it. For the woman teaching the seminar,
that may have been a time when she should have chosen to be
aggressive and to have contained her desire to draw others close.
Such behavior would have benefited her on two counts: She would
have met her boss's expectations, and she might have been more
effective with her students. Even adult students expect a teacher to
know more about the subject at hand and to be of a higher rank in
the classroom.

Gilligan uses the image of the web and the hierarchy to describe
the varying preferences of men and women. For men, the ideal is
to be alone at the top; their fear is that others will draw too close.
Women see the hierarchy as unstable and unequal. They prefer to
be at the center of the web, connected with others; danger lurks in
being too far out on the edge, away from others. That distinction

may account, in part, for the greater ease men feel in organizations which are hierarchical. And yet it is not the whole explanation. No organization is a rigid hierarchy. Denise Cavanaugh, a management consultant with Capital Gains, Inc., in Washington, D.C., uses the image of a jungle gym to describe the structure of organizations. "Organizations are neither webs nor ladders," she says, "but jungle gyms, which to my mind combines those two. A ladder is two-dimensional—you either go up or down. But a jungle gym is a combination of ladders, tubes, circles, and slides. Men love jungle gyms because they are ladder-like. You can climb up and down and dodge around, in one side and out the other side."

Jungle gyms are a little like webs, too, but that doesn't mean women are at ease with them. The difficulty women sometimes face in fitting into corporate structures is not as simple as just being uncomfortable with a hierarchical structure. When a woman approaches the workplace she is often less confident than a man might be; she is anxious about her chances of success and eager to make the right moves. The early message girls receive is to behave: Get A's in school, sit up straight, fold your hands in your lap—do it right. As Cavanaugh explains: "The issue here is that men look at jungle gyms and know that they can dodge and hide and move around. A woman looks at a jungle gym and says, 'Where do I start?,' 'Where do I go second?,' 'How will I know whether I am doing it right?' Men climb around, talk to each other and pick up the rules." Women, of course, can learn to do the same, particularly—yes, you're hearing it again—if they cultivate some aggressiveness.

MEN AND AGGRESSION

Male bonds often are not based on deep personal knowledge of one another, but on concern with the dynamics of the group and with establishing a pecking order among the men. How does this group of men, however small, function together? How is it organized? Who is the leader? Those are questions women seldom ask about their groups. Women see aggression as a threat to the bonds they have with others, and they are less inclined to be aggressive.

Women choose not to dominate, less because they are passive or compliant or powerless than because they lack the psychological drive to dominate. For women, egalitarian relationships—the web instead of the ladder—are the ideal. Men, however, are compelled to rehearse their masculinity, to confirm it again and again by exerting their control and domination over others.

Nowhere is that impulse more evident than in work relationships. The business world is organized—by men—in a way that makes it possible for participants to measure their achievements against those of others and to establish their positions in the hierarchy.

Women in business sometimes use a people-oriented style that does not reinforce positions in the hierarchy. Although such a style may be successful in achieving results or meeting business objectives, it may still fail to impress men, who admire aggression. Denise Cavanaugh was consulting for an accounting firm when she noticed that one CPA, a woman, had not been sent to Chicago to do an audit that appeared to be her responsibility. Cavanaugh asked the head of the firm why he hadn't sent the woman. Was there something wrong with her skills? The man was reticent and replied, "I don't know. She's just not right for the job."

When pressed, he finally said, "Well, when she gets to Chicago she'll go up to the people and say, 'We'd like to do an audit, could you prepare a room for us and have all your records ready by Monday?' I don't want her to say that. I want her to say, 'We're here to do an audit. We want all your records in sixty minutes, we want four phones, and three secretaries.' " The style he knew the woman would use did not project the image he wanted for his firm, nor did it impress him as being effective. Her intention may have been to be firm and direct, but the message that came across to her male boss was weak. "We have to translate what we say," says Cavanaugh, "so that men can hear what we intend." Had the woman accountant understood male psychology, she might have been aware of her boss's desire that she project a more aggressive image and she might have been more effective in displaying the firmness she surely felt, while still operating in a way that was most comfortable to her. That was, again, an opportunity for a woman to choose to demonstrate the aggressive, take-charge behavior her boss would admire, not directed at him, but at others.

Although men do not have the intense desire women do to organize their lives around relationships with others, men do have a strong need to connect with other men. Their need is seldom for intimate connections, but rather those that revolve around rivalry, dominance, and aggression. It is a powerful drive and one that frequently guides the actions of men.

A MAN AMONG MEN

Boys are strongly influenced by their playmates. Although girls seem to display greater intimacy with friends of their own sex—and have the reputation for being the social sex—boys are more gregarious in the number of playmates they have and are more susceptible to peer influence. In one study, for instance, boys were asked whether they would go to a camp that would be more interesting, but where they didn't know anyone, or would they prefer to go to the camp where their friends were going. Boys generally choose to go with their friends. In studies where children are asked to rate each other according to various criteria, boys are most often mentioned as the classmates who go along with what the other children are doing.

That gang mentality extends into adulthood. Males tend to pay close attention to their own sex. Given the choice, some men will always select another man as a companion. One young man, a Republican, tells of his experience serving on a three-person commission with two Democrats, one male and one female, both in their late fifties. The young man was surprised when the older man on the board sought him out. The Democrat, a high school graduate, car salesman, former military man elected "by the good old boys in the Knights of Columbus Hall,'' would seem to have little in common with the Republican thirty years his junior who had three college degrees. Nonetheless, he befriended him rather than align with the female commissioner, who was closer to his age and politics. ''I didn't agree with 90 percent of what he thought,'' says the young man, ''but we had a decent enough relationship. He needed somebody to talk to and he couldn't establish any kind of personal relationship with her.''

That the need of men to bond with one another is fundamental to masculinity is an idea the social scientist Lionel Tiger popularized. Tiger sees the male bonding need as essential and universal among men, just as the needs for sex, food, and shelter are.

Tiger contends, in *Men in Groups*, that men need to bond with other men in order to fully experience maleness. He says that socializing with other males is both satisfying and energizing to men, and that it necessarily involves the *exclusion* of women. As evidence of the distinct and particular need of men to bond, Tiger cites the tendency throughout history for men to form secret societies and other single-sex groups, a behavior women almost never engage in. Tiger says secret societies in particular are ''oddly primitive'' and are essentially aggressive groups that deliberately invite hostility and fear from those excluded.

Men seem to need groups that are separate from women; they need to be with other men in order to refuel their masculinity. Writer Paul Theroux expresses the ambivalence many men today seem to have about women and about male separateness from women. ''I have always disliked being a man,'' he writes, because of the ''terrible ambition of manliness,'' which ''insists on difference and connives at superiority . . . masculinity celebrates the exclusive company of men. That is why it is so grotesque; and that is also why there is no manliness without inadequacy—because it denies men the natural friendship of women.''

Although most men today are not members of secret societies, there is still an exclusivity in their relationships—even in the workplace—that is unlike the relationships women have with one another.

Shunning Weakness and Emotion

The excessive importance many men place on being strong and aggressive is part of manliness, but it requires denying any emotion that conveys weakness or vulnerability. Jean Baker Miller says that men tend to fear and hate weakness and "to try to get rid of it immediately and sometimes frantically." Because no one is invulnerable, trying to be so denies an important aspect of human experience. Miller considers the superior ability of women to admit to feelings of weakness or vulnerability to be a strength. Those are emotions that are generated in everyone; only by experiencing them, Miller notes, can a person truly grow.

In *Toward a New Psychology of Women* she describes a case where a man developed physical problems after receiving a promotion that he wanted but feared. Miller explains that his refusal to talk to his wife about it was a result of the male abhorrence of weakness and helplessness. He wanted, above all, to face everything in life feeling "like a man"—always strong, always competent. "Anything less he experienced as a threat to his manliness. Such a requirement is unrealistic in the extreme, for we face repeated challenges in life; we are sure to feel doubts all along."

Displays of emotion on the job are particularly abhorrent to men. While some events in personal life inevitably provoke emotion, work is the place where men want most to be strong, competent, invulnerable. And yet because work usually requires close association with others and frequently generates pressure, intense emotion can easily come into the workplace. Negative emotions, such as frustration, fear, bewilderment, jealousy, and resentment, turn up frequently and are the most difficult to deal with.

The dichotomy in how the sexes view emotion is especially evident in nurturing fields like medicine. And women sometimes suffer for being unable or unwilling to deny their emotions on the job. One woman, for example, when she was in medical school, received a final examination grade equal to that of a male classmate, but he was given an A for the course and she received a C. The reason cited was that the woman got too emotionally involved with her patients—a negative trait from the point of view of male physicians. The woman persisted, nonetheless, and without giving up her sometimes passionate involvement with patients, became a successful pediatrician.

Men are seldom revealing in their emotions and often have a limited range of feelings they can express. Denied to them are grief, guilt, sadness, fear, tenderness, joy, even interest, except when it is related to power. Men can, for example, show interest in subjects like sports, politics, machinery, and cars, because those help fill the need they have for dominance assertion. Anything else, males learn from an early age to shun. Society makes it not only unacceptable, but dangerous for males to express emotions that indicate any vulnerability. If they reveal an inability to control their emotions, they risk getting beat up in the schoolyard, being admonished by their parents and others to be "big boys," and, later, losing out on important positions at work. Tough men are deemed worthy of the big assignments; weak men (and women) are not.

The One Emotion Men Can Show

Males learn from their upbringing that at least one emotion is permitted them: anger. Because that's the only expression available, men tend to interpret every powerful or negative emotion they have as anger. Psychologist Narayan Singh Khalsa says that men don't have intermediate behavior with which to handle complicated emotions or vulnerable situations. "They have only the equipment of a child or a retarded person to deal with difficult emotional situations," he says. "They are, in fact, emotionally retarded."

Khalsa says a typical emotional response used by men is the "black stomp." That's when a man rages around, in a display of dominance, perhaps literally stomping his feet. What it means is that he is overwhelmed. Although he may be feeling more frustration or fear than anger, he only knows how to reveal the anger. In an odd twist of logic and language, men who display anger—even in frequent or uncontrolled episodes—are not considered "emotional" by other men. That's a pejorative reserved for those, usually women, who display sympathy or vulnerability.

The widespread use men make of anger, an emotion women display sparingly (though often just as ineffectively as men do), is confusing to women. For a woman to express anger, she must be very angry. Just as crying is a significant event for a man, displaying anger is a major happening for a woman. Women have to be careful not to interpret male anger in the same light as female anger; they risk giving men's anger more meaning than it merits.

By attributing to men's anger more significance than it deserves, you do two things: You give men a powerful weapon, in particular an easy way to bully subordinates; and you suffer unnecessary emotional stress. Men usually recover from their explosions of anger much more quickly than the women who are witnesses or objects of the anger. An hour after a rancorous outburst, a man may be fully recovered and speaking to you in a normal tone of voice as if nothing happened; you, however, may still be hurt, angry, and waiting for the strength to update your résumé.

To keep from overreacting to men's anger, you must learn to interpret the emotion in different ways. A man's anger may be directed at you—he may be pointing his finger at you, using your name, shouting in your direction—but try to remember that he is exhibiting learned behavior. He may be merely trying to get a point across by saying, "Look, I'm serious about this." Or he might mean, "I'm out of control; because I don't know how to deal with this, I'm getting angry so you'll know to back off and not bother me until I figure it out." He may truly be angry or have some good reason to be displeased, of course; you just have to remember that he is expressing his displeasure in a way that may not be easy for you to cope with and may be out of proportion to the problem according to your standards.

Learn to discount men's anger—even when you know a man may

have good reason to be vexed—and keep reminding yourself that men's anger is different from yours. Denise Cavanaugh tells this story about French fruit vendors as a way of helping women to remember to discount the anger of American men: In France it is not customary to pick out your own fruit at a market; the merchant puts in a bag what you point to. An American woman who didn't know that went to France and brought on the wrath of a fruit vendor when she touched the produce. He shouted, waved his arms, and got red in the face. In that situation, the woman knew how to deal with the anger; she didn't get upset (and in fact was amused). She knew enough to factor in cultural differences while listening to the Frenchman's anger; she knew the French can be more ardent in their expression than Americans. She listened to the anger, discounted it by at least half, and bought her fruit when he calmed down. What women have to do when faced with men's anger at home is to learn to think: "I'm living in a cross-cultural world; I am in France buying fruit and I'm faced with a French fruit vendor who is crazed because I touched his peaches. I will listen to his anger, but discount it."

Even when you are able to discount the anger, you may need to get away from the enraged man in order to cope with your own feelings. By physically getting away from his outburst, you can more easily determine what you think about the problem that brought on the anger. You might say to him, "You've had your outburst, now I need a few minutes to react, too." Then walk around for twenty minutes, or go into your office and give yourself a chance to think objectively and to calm down. Many women react physically to male anger with an involuntary fear response—elevated blood pressure, flushed face, constricted bowels. If that happens to you, you need some time to talk yourself out of the reaction. The more calm, rational, and objective you can be in the face of his wrath, the better off you are.

The other side of the anger issue is that while women need to learn to discount male anger, they must also learn to express their own. A woman can be effective in boldly displaying her displeasure and anger, saying, "I'm serious about this; I'm upset by what happened." Consider these moves: stand when you're angry and want to say something; develop an ominous expression and an angry tone of voice; don't be afraid to point (at people, if necessary), or occasionally throw something for emphasis, or rip up a memo or report and toss it in the wastebasket if that's the object of your displeasure. Because men are accustomed to using anger themselves, they'll understand when you use it.

LISTENING TO MEN

The narrow range of male emotional expression and the limited experience men have with a variety of emotions may dull their sensitivity to the emotional life around them, including that of the workplace. Women readily recognize the role emotions play at work. Says one: "Emotions are a part of being human. You can't lobotomize your emotions when you walk in the office every day." But men are less able—and less willing—than women to recognize and cope with their own emotions and those of others. Another woman says the men she works with seem unaware of how others around them are reacting or feeling about what's going on. "I don't know whether that's self-protection or not wanting to feel emotion," she says. One man in her office frequently offends others at work. "We have a good relationship; we have drinks together and talk about sports and music and the things that interest us. But when he deals with others, I can see him being totally insensitive to their ego needs. It's hard for him to understand why others get angry with him. We talk about it, but ultimately he always believes he's right and that people should do what he asks. He just can't recognize that others need to be stroked and patted and included in his plans."

Men are not emotionless, of course; their lives often provoke strong and painful feelings, but those emotions are seldom put into words, examined, or, ultimately, experienced. When men do have problems that can't be ignored, they often turn to women, not to men, for help. That's as true in the workplace as in personal life. Men find women to be better listeners, to have more sophisticated understanding of emotions and relationships. But there's an additional reason that applies especially at work: Men are most concerned about maintaining their image of invulnerability for the benefit of other men. They will, at times, let down their guard around women.

Women tell moving stories about men whose suffering in their personal lives affects them at work. Patricia, a research psychologist now working in a large company in the energy industry, has on a number of occasions been approached by men she works with who have deep personal secrets to share. One man's wife was dying of lung cancer, and he would periodically go into Patricia's office, close the door, and talk about it. "I don't think he had anyone else to talk to, even friends," she says. Another man and his wife were trying unsuccessfully to have children, and he would talk to Patricia about that. Others have approached her on their frustrations with bosses and confusion over career goals. They don't talk to their male colleagues about those problems and concerns. "They can't," says Patricia. "This is a competitive, compulsive, never-give-an-inch business. To admit to such problems would be to admit to vulnerability."

The fact that men will turn to female colleagues seems to put women in a position that is plainly unfair: Women cannot express their feelings and problems to men without risking being seen as weak and overly emotional. And yet women must be receptive to men when they wish to reveal emotions, for in most circumstances, turning away a man who seeks to confide would be a mistake—both morally and politically. Holding those two positions at once would seem to put women in a self-effacing role, but that's not the case. And fairness is not the issue here. The issue is, instead, that women must take advantage of their own psychological attributes—and chief among these is their capacity for sympathy and understanding—and at the same time recognize that men see emotional displays (other than anger) from women as signs of weakness.

Being unable to discuss personal problems at work is not a great loss to most women, who generally have many people—friends and family—to confide in. In any case, unburdening yourself at work to men or women is usually a mistake, for reasons that go beyond what men think of emotional displays. The less colleagues know about your personal life, the better. If men want to talk to you, however, use—don't deny—your sophisticated understanding of emotions. It can help you build alliances with men and gain their trust.

Madelyn Jennings of Gannett considers sensitivity to other people's lives, personal problems, and job stress to be one of the characteristics of successful women. "This is not to suggest that women should become the Mother Confessors of the executive suite," she says. "But I think women who are successful are not cold fish and have some empathy for the personal problems or job stresses of others. They are outside themselves enough to be able to be interested in others. That builds bridges. Lots of times men are too protective to allow something that is hurting them to show to other men." They may show it to a woman, however, and she can command their respect by adroitly handling their emotional expressions—as well as her own. Showing men that you understand them and their problems and that you can be trusted is an important step in making men comfortable working with women.

PART TWO

WORKING WITH MEN

7 MAKING MEN COMFORTABLE

"A woman in the job has to deliver everything that a man has to, but there are barriers to her delivery—especially the comfort barrier. Despite a lot of progress, men still are not entirely comfortable with women in business," says Carolyn Carter of Grey Advertising. "You cannot remove a fact of life from the business environment: Men relate more comfortably to men and women relate better to women."

Women and men agree that it's simply easier to deal with your own sex than to figure out the mysteries of the opposite one. When working with someone of your own sex, communication is often quicker; less effort and energy overall is required. Though it may be easier for women to build alliances with other women, that solidarity isn't enough. Women must build alliances with men in order to be effective in business.

AT EASE

A woman in her thirties who works for a small manufacturing business says, "I feel that men judge me, that they want something from me, and I just can't relax around them."

Her feelings are shared by many women, but learning to relax around men is a vital first step you must take in learning to build strong work relationships with men. In order to make men comfortable with you, you have to be comfortable with them. Ray Siehndel, a lawyer and businessman, describes a woman he deals with and admires as intelligent, confident, always prepared, and "secure enough that she's relaxed. That's what puts me off about women sometimes; they aren't relaxed. But this woman seems comfortable around men; she seems comfortable with her position, and she seems comfortable about knowing what she's doing. That makes me comfortable."

The kind of poise and confidence that puts others at ease was demonstrated to Madelyn Jennings of Gannett by another woman executive in the firm. At a staff meeting led by a male manager, an issue the woman was responsible for arose. The manager earlier had requested a change in an advertisement and wanted to know whether it had been made. The woman had set the change in motion, but hadn't followed up and couldn't confirm it. She left the meeting room to get a copy of the now-published ad. In she came and sure enough, there had been a slipup—the change had not been effected. "There was fire coming out of the manager's nostrils and ears and everything else," says Jennings. "This was a major goof." As he looked at the ad, tension mounted around the silent group of ten people. For a few seconds, the woman who had made the mistake endured the silence, then said, "Please, get it over with. I can't take this anymore," and she slumped in her chair with mock despair. At once the tension in the room began to ease. "Instead of sitting there like a little girl waiting for her daddy to rap her fanny," says Jennings, "she said, 'I can't stand the suspense.' "

With her touch of humor she let the manager know she realized she had made a significant error, but also that she thought the problem wasn't worth starting World War III over. The woman knew she had made a mistake and, for a professional, no further punishment is necessary. Had she been less poised and sputtered, "I'm sorry, gee, I told him, I meant to, I thought," she would have made herself look worse. Had she waited quietly for the manager to speak, she would have showed she expected punishment; instead her actions diffused the tension of a tough situation and saved her relationship with the manager.

Women have to learn to be at case in a variety of situations, not all of which require such quick thinking. Many are the ongoing, everyday encounters with men on which good business relationships are built.

Judy, a product manager for a medical equipment company in Denver, travels the country meeting customers (who are almost always men) to find out how they're using her company's equipment and what their needs and problems are. If those men don't feel easy with her, they won't open up and tell her what she needs to know. She employs the simplest of how-to-win-friends-and-influence-people techniques: She finds out what matters to them. "Men in particular," she says, "like you to talk about what is important to them—whether it's their cash-flow problems or sports. I've found that you don't have to know a lot of details, just enough to let them know you're willing to listen."

Judy also tries to relax her own style a bit. Like many women, she sometimes hides behind a formal demeanor. "I know I can be too businesslike, and can rely too much on knowledge," she says. "Sometimes I can feel the tone around me change because I've started to lecture. You can't develop much of a relationship if you're lecturing and distant. And people aren't going to tell you what you need to know—they're going to tell you what you want to hear."

Mothers, Lovers, Sisters, Secretaries

One reason women have to tread carefully around men is that nearly every professional working woman is a pioneer. She's teaching men to see women in a new way, whether she—or he—recognizes it. Most men are new at relating to women as peers on the job or in their personal lives. Men, however, are accustomed to women being in subordinate positions. They know how to give a woman an order, but are far less comfortable asking her opinion and, least of all, taking an order from her.

"Men still see women in traditional roles," says Meredith Fern-strom, senior vice president at American Express. "There still aren't very many women in corporations, particularly in any large numbers in management ranks. So the women that most men tend to associate with are either their mothers or their wives or girlfriends or their secretaries. There are far fewer women who are on a peer or certainly on a superior level.''

A young man in the Midwest described the problems one of his male colleagues was having relating to a woman co-worker his own age: ''It might have been a little different for him if she'd been ten years older; he might have forgiven her behavior some. Or if she had been younger, he might have looked upon her as someone he might be interested in; if she was a *lot* younger, maybe someone he could look upon with a little fatherly something.'' Contending with her as a peer apparently was not an option.

Many men simply don't have any experience working with women. Asked about women in his company, one man from a large corporation said, ''There aren't enough of them to make any difference; they don't affect the decision-making process; they're all at low-middle management positions and none of them are really in a position of influence.'' Another executive, groping for something to say about the women under him, remembered that there was a female manager who reported to one of the department heads who, in turn, reported to him: ''She's a very tough kind of woman—I'm told. Now, she doesn't come across that way too much to me, but other people who deal with her in the department say so; she's considered hard to work for.'' This man had had no firsthand experience with her, or with any other women managers, on which to base his opinions, only hearsay.

One woman attorney who went to work for a two-man law firm found herself in a difficult position because the partners didn't know how to treat her. She was the first woman lawyer they had ever hired; all the other women who had worked for them were secretaries. ''They didn't quite know what to do with me. I wasn't young enough to be a daughter and I wasn't old enough to be a wife. And I was more sophisticated than a secretary,'' she says. ''They never quite got a fix on me.''

Drivers and Dabblers

Because men have little professional experience with women, they have difficulty understanding how varied the species is. Some men, particularly those in the higher ranks of corporations, tend to see working women as falling into two groups. There's the hard-driving, single woman, who is a particular enigma; she is not only difficult for men to understand and relate to, but sometimes resented. One man remarked about a single woman superior to him: "She stays down there at the office all night mucking around, trying to stir up trouble. She hasn't got another goddamn thing on God's green earth to do."

Then there's the dabbler, the woman who works for amusement. Men can understand that easily enough because that's often how they see their wives and the wives of their colleagues. The dabbler perhaps enjoys working, but she gives it up willingly if she finds a man who can support her. More significant, this is a woman who *assumes* that men's careers are more important than her own.

Even men in their twenties, thirties, and forties don't necessarily have much experience with women who are serious about their careers. If their wives do work, their careers are secondary to the men's. A woman in her late twenties who works in finance announced she was getting married, and the first question one of the top-ranking executives, a man in his mid-forties, asked was, "Are you going to continue working?" His wife didn't work and apparently he didn't expect other men's wives to either. A twenty-two-year-old MBA student, married to a woman with an undergraduate degree, says he and his wife have "old-fashioned" roles in their marriage. His wife is working part time while he's in school because they need the money, but he suspects that even after he gets a job she'll continue to work part time, to avoid being "bored and lonely." Neither of them expect her to have a career.

The way men view the women they encounter at work is severely limited by their experiences with women in their personal lives.

Women professionals tend to marry someone their level or higher, but men either marry women in jobs equal or below theirs—or, most likely, they marry women who have not opted for the work world. The higher up a man is and the more money he makes, the less likely his wife is to work. According to surveys done by the executive search firm of Korn/Ferry International, 95 percent of male executives are married, and 86 percent of those are married to women who don't work outside the home. The situation for female executives is just the opposite. Of those who are married (and only 41 percent are), 82 percent have husbands who work full time.

Working women who are serious about their careers, who expect the same opportunities for advancement and challenging assignments that men do, are something strange and hard to fathom for many men. Such a man continually adjusts his views of the women he meets at work. She isn't like my wife, or is she? Is she the sisterly type? Why isn't she home taking care of her kids like my mother did me? That division doesn't exist in his view of men, of course. The guy in the next office is very likely a husband and father and potential weekend golfing mate, all of which makes it easier for a man to relate to him and understand him.

The lives of executive women, however, are not so easily understood by men. Meredith Fernstrom left a job in Washington, D.C., with the U.S. Department of Commerce to join American Express in New York. Her husband continues to live and work in Washington and the two commute on weekends. An unusual arrangement, no question about it, but it especially puzzles some of her male colleagues. "There are some men here," says Fernstrom, "who almost every conversation I have will say something like 'Oh, are you still commuting? How's it going? I don't see how you do it.' I think to them it's sort of an intriguing thing personally as much as anything, because they can't imagine their wives ever doing it or having it in their marriages."

The more two people have in common—whether it's the same hometown, a shared enthusiasm for basketball, children of the same ages—the easier it is for them to connect with one another. Finding common ground with men often isn't easy for women if they search their personal lives. But any women can rely on the shared interests that working in the same business brings. One woman who frequently travels to trade shows and conventions, representing her company's products, says she finds that men are often confused by her presence. "I feel them looking at me like, 'Well, whose girlfriend or secretary or wife are you?' And some are visibly shocked to find I'm a professional person with a lot of knowledge about their business," she says. "Once they learn that, though, they usually relax and are more comfortable."

The Matter of Age

The age of a man is less determinant of his attitudes toward women than might be expected. Younger as well as older men present certain problems and opportunities for women.

The obvious difficulty women encounter with older men is that they can be the most traditional of all in their attitudes toward women. Many were brought up assuming women would always take a backseat and they are genuinely baffled by today's ambitious young women. They simply don't have in their realm of experience anything to help them relate to women who are or aspire to be high-powered. A woman who was a nursing supervisor encountered most of her problems with older male doctors. "They grew up in an age when men were very much dominant and physicians were certainly revered," she says. "It wasn't very long ago that nurses gave up their chairs for physicians to sit down, called them sir, and did *anything* they asked. That's changed and some men have found that change difficult to adapt to."

Working with an older man can be easiest for a woman when he's higher ranking. That's because the arrangement meets the expectations of everyone involved. That is, the man is likely to be most comfortable being superior to a woman and both are likely to expect the boss to be older.

Age is a definer of roles and causes problems mainly when it doesn't work the way we expect it to. If, for example, you are the same age as those ahead of you, you may be perceived as a threat, as someone breathing down the necks of your superiors. The same problem occurs between same-age peers—age isn't helping define positions and thus a woman is apt to appear threatening. If your boss is older he's less likely to view you as a threat because his seniority keeps you from being seen as an equal.

The big problem for women comes when they are bosses to older or same-age men. Carolyn Carter, who has risen quickly at Grey Advertising and been promoted over older men, is in her early thirties. She says she knows there have been men who report to her who have thought: "Oh, no. Not only am I going to have to work for a woman—I'm going to have to work for a *girl*." When age works as an equalizer, a woman has to strive all the harder to maintain and strengthen her position in the hierarchy.

BEING A BOSS AMONG MEN

At one time, all the account supervisors at the ad agency who report to Carter were men. "There were days when I felt like Barbara Stanwyck in the 'Big Valley' and I was running the ranch," she says. Her supervisors even jokingly referred to themselves as "Carolyn's boys."

With each man who has reported to her, Carter says she has not "had the benefit of the assumption"—the assumption being that she has the smarts and ability that go with her position. With each of her "boys," the unspoken—and even sometimes spoken—challenge has been, "Okay, I've heard you're good, now *prove* it to me."

"If they worked for a man, they would assume credibility, but since I'm a woman I have to prove it. I've seen this happen time after time," she says. "I've been 100 percent successful, but 100 percent of the time that barrier has been there."

To break down the barrier, there's no substitute for being good at what you do. Carter says she lets her performance show the men who work for her that she's capable and should be supervising them because she's more knowledgeable than they. Her second tactic is to demonstrate that the men can benefit from her competence. She lets them know she'll be their cheerleader, will help them do their best, and, most important, will let their stars shine.

Meredith Fernstrom, who became a senior vice president at American Express when she was in her mid-thirties, also was promoted over older men. "The women my age and younger who are moving up in corporations are going to face some difficult relationships when they have men reporting to them," she says. "The attitude is: 'How could she be better than me? Number one, she's a woman, and number two, she's younger than I am and hasn't been here as long.' It's a threat to anyone, male or female, when you see a younger person moving up and getting higher responsibilities."

Fernstrom handles it by being as professional and objective as she can. "I try to bring those people in to let them know that I was put in that position to do a job and that my supervisors have a lot of confidence in my ability to do it. I let them know everyone has a contribution to make—and I expect them to make theirs. You have to maintain a certain degree of authority and firmness. I don't think you can let go of that position you're in and become just one of the guys operating at their level."

Women who supervise both men and women report that they need different skills for each sex. Men not only are more likely to challenge a woman's authority; they also can be more demanding than women. Daniela Kuper, an entrepreneur in Boulder, Colorado, has several people employed in her business, some of whom are men. "The women who work for me tend to make as little trouble for me as possible," she says, "it's really wonderful. They say, 'I took care of that' and 'How are you today?' But the men! They require more energy. They have no problem asserting themselves and saying what they want and questioning policy."

Males are used to being in the limelight; beginning as children, boys get more attention from adults. Boys tend not only to be encouraged more than girls, but also to be punished more often. Experts aren't sure why that happens. Eleanor Maccoby and Carol Jacklin (*The Psychology of Sex Differences*) say that adults respond as if they find boys more interesting and more attention provoking than girls. They suggest that perhaps boys are valued more or that their greater strength and aggressiveness require that they be better schooled than girls in social behavior. Whatever the explanation, those pressures lead little boys, who become men, to expect plenty of attention.

No matter how good a woman boss may be or how adept she is at demonstrating her competence or providing adequate attention, however, some men can't accept a woman's authority. Daniela Kuper found that out when she hired a male designer for her ad agency. She says her problems with him were "very much a man/woman thing." He questioned her authority repeatedly.

"After he had worked here for about a week, he felt free to lay into me," she says. "He would tell me things like: 'You know, you have a tremendous ego. Do you have any idea how big your ego is? You have a inflated opinion of yourself.' He would just keep digging into me. I know he would never have done that to a man."

Kuper says she thinks he had trouble working for a woman because he didn't have a very good opinion of himself or of women. Reporting to a woman "made him look bad in his own eyes," she says. He didn't have a strong enough hold on his masculinity to tolerate the threat that working for a woman posed. No amount of reassurance can make such a man happy to take orders from a woman. Finally, Kuper did what any boss would do with a repeated offender who showed no signs of rehabilitation: She fired him.

REPORTING TO A MALE BOSS

The advantage of being the boss, of course, is that you *can* fire the impossible-to-work-with men. When you're the subordinate, however, all your efforts must be directed at working well with your boss. The essential first step is to build confidence and trust. A woman must convince her male boss that she is an asset, not a threat or a problem. To do that she must first deliver professionally; her work must be of high quality, delivered on time; it must reflect good thinking and be strategically on target time after time. That's the primary basis for trust. Beyond that, personal rapport, loyalty, attitude, and all the intangibles that build good relationships among colleagues contribute to a woman's success with a male boss.

Even though the male boss/female subordinate is the easiest of relationships for most men, women sometimes find themselves working for men who can't accept a woman, under any circumstances, on professional terms. When that happens, a woman's only solution may be to find herself another boss.

That's what Donna, a computer programmer for a large corporation, finally did. For a number of years she worked for a man who she thinks deliberately held her back. He repeatedly refused to promote her and also refused her requests for lateral transfers; she was useful to him right where she was. She had followed the first line of action in her efforts to get ahead: She did her work well. That's the right course when working with most men, but this one was different. "He had a low opinion of women," Donna says. "He didn't know how to deal with those who were competent. He wanted to believe that the women in the office weren't capable of doing a good job and when he had women working for him who were, he didn't quite know what to do about it." Once Donna figured that out, she went around her boss to another supervisor who agreed to hire her away—and promote her in the process.

Another woman, Cynthia, once worked for a man who saw her as a threat. She says she discovered it was a no-win situation when she realized that if she did her job well and showed herself to be worthy of a promotion, he would see that not as strong performance, but as a threat. And she clearly couldn't do less than her best just to please him. When she tried to get to know him better and help him to see her as a valued member of the group, she hit a dead end.

Critical to success and advancement is knowing when you're in a no-win situation. "If you don't take aggressive steps to get out of it, you can wallow and lose *years*," says Cynthia. She took the most aggressive of steps and went to her boss's boss to explain that she could not do her best work in her current situation. Her tactic worked. And she ended up confirming her boss's worst fears. She got his job.

It seems a paradox that women, who are supposed to be "good with people" and who place more significance on good relationships with others, have a harder time than men building camaraderie at work. In a study conducted by Kay Deaux of Purdue University, male and female managers in a retail store rated their own job performance in several categories. Deaux found that males rated themselves higher on having a good relationship with their superiors—all males. The supervisors also rated the men higher than the women on that score. Deaux reports that male managers not only had a better relationship but received more approval for their work. Her conclusion is what many working women have learned on their own: The informal networks where instruction and encouragement of efforts occur are not as easily accessible to women. A woman who wants to get ahead needs to do something about that.

ONE CONQUEST AT A TIME

The best way for a woman to build the relationships with men that will help her to progress and do her job well is to start creating her own peer network. And the most effective way to do that is one man at a time. A woman can't take on all her male colleagues at once, but if she makes an effort to get to know one at a time, eventually there will be a number of men throughout the company who know her and are comfortable with her.

Dealing with men one-to-one is always easiest. You can judge the individual; you can see his reactions and respond to them without the additional concerns of the dynamics of the group. "One-to-one is easier; it's just person-to-person," says one of very few females in an engineering company. "The only time I think of men as a group, as being all alike, is when they *are* in a group. That's when they're hardest to deal with.''

MEN IN GROUPS

The strongest threat to a woman in a gathering where she is far outnumbered by men is not that she'll be deliberately shut out or that the men will pick on her. The threat is that she'll be *invisible*. A woman can fade into the background in a pack of men because of the intense activity that goes on among them. If the group is new, the men will be busy establishing a pecking order; if it is not they'll be busy acknowledging the old one, testing positions, and playing to one another. We tend to think of women as group oriented and social, but it is males who most need their groups—and it's other males they want to gang with.

One of the myths about sex differences that Maccoby and Jacklin dispel in *The Psychology of Sex Differences* is that girls are more social than boys. They found instead that both sexes are interested in social stimuli and respond to social reinforcement. They did find, however, a difference in kind if not degree. Boys tend to congregate in large groups, whereas girls are more likely to gather in two's and three's. The size of those social groups may have something to do with male dominance patterns. Small groups don't generally need a dominance hierarchy to function well, but large groups do. When little boys—or big boys—gather, they joust and tilt to establish each participant's slot in the hierarchy.

Research shows, for example, that there's no difference in the amount of activity boys and girls exhibit when they play alone, and when girls are joined by other girls their level of activity stays pretty much the same. But when little boys gang together they spring to life, engaging in far more activity than when they are alone. Their play is often boisterous, competitive, and aggressively physical rough-and-tumble. It is a prelude to the backslapping and verbal rough-and-tumble they'll engage in with other men when they grow up.

In business groups, such as at meetings, men are more concerned with the behavior of other men than with the behavior of women. They look at other men more, cut off women's sentences, acknowledge other men, and build on their ideas in a way they don't with women. The verbal and nonverbal communication keeps winding the circle tighter and tighter around the men, leaving women out. That doesn't mean women can't get in the discussion; it just means they must work harder to do so.

Meredith Fernstrom says she is aware that men tend to dominate meetings and that women have a harder time getting their statements on the table. "Men tend to interrupt more," she says, "and women are more complacent about that than they should be. I think we tend to err on the side of acceptance or complacency, so we don't come across on the other extreme as being seen as bossy or too aggressive." When it happens to her and she becomes aware that she's not getting equal time, she persists until her points are made.

Carolyn Carter also finds that in groups she must work harder than men do to maintain a strong role in the activities, relying on her expertise and making sure she has an important role to play in a meeting. "And I'm pleasant," she says. "That makes people more willing to listen—and makes me more effective."

Although a woman cannot permit herself to be left out of business discussions that are vital to her getting the job done, at times she may have to accept being left out of more informal and social situations. A woman can get promoted and do her job effectively without playing golf, but she can't do so without playing an active role in business meetings.

OUTSIDE THE BUDDY NETWORK

Women often think that the way to get ahead is to take advantage of social situations that will get them into the informal networks where business information is shared. Because who you know and who your buddies are *is* important to getting ahead, it seems only sensible to nurture social relationships with colleagues and bosses.

The difficulty for women, however, is that the social networks don't necessarily work so well for them as they do for men. The same behavior from a woman and a man doesn't always receive a similar interpretation. When Donna, the computer programmer, started a new job, she joined a group of colleagues and superiors who were accustomed to going out for a drink after work on Fridays. The group was made up of a few women but mostly men, a few at Donna's level and some at her boss's and the next highest grade in the company. It seemed the perfect situation to get to know the higher-ups who could be beneficial to her career. But the results were far from what she expected.

The young men at Donna's level who were part of this group came to be seen as the up-and-comers. They were pushed into high-profile assignments, gained recognition, and were promoted, sometimes into other divisions of the company to work for friends of the male bosses who were in the social group.

What Donna got from those Friday evenings out, however, was not a desirable assignment but an embarrassing offer to be set up for a date with one of the boss's friends. "It didn't take me long to realize that although my peers accepted my being there," she says, "the people at my boss's level treated me as if I were looking to pick up a guy. Eventually, I quit socializing with them."

Donna could see that there was a network of men who had worked together over the years for the company, moving from city to city and division to division, and that they traded employees back and forth, promoting and advancing the careers of younger workers. But she couldn't get in. "I was excluded from that," says Donna. "There was something going on there that we women just weren't a part of."

The buddy networks exist at all levels, perhaps becoming even tighter and more exclusive higher up. Congresswoman Patricia Schroeder of Colorado said in an interview with *U.S. News and World Report* that even after six terms in the House she lacks the access to power and networks she'd like to have. "As a woman in Washington," she says, "I cannot go down to the Democratic Club . . . and tip a few drinks with the lobbyists. I suppose I could, but it would be real sticky. When it's time to donate money for the next campaign, the lobbyists tend to give to their buddies, and their buddies tend to be the ones they socialize with after hours or go fishing with up on the Eastern Shore of Maryland or Virginia. They really don't know what to do with us [women] . . . We still are a society where men and women are yet to be really good friends, and that carries over.''

Even if a woman is invited, her participation is likely to be different from that of the men's. One young sales representative who travels a lot with the men in her company, shares common interests, and generally has a good relationship with them, says she is still left out of many all-male activities. ''No one, even in that congenial group, makes any attempt to say, 'Well sure, you could come with us,' because I *can't*. Even if I did go to play racketball with them I wouldn't be playing at the same level they do, and it wouldn't be the same as what goes on between them on the court.''

The impossibility of participating fully with male colleagues was pointed out most vividly for the same woman at a sales conference in Nevada. She had spent the evening with a group of men from other companies, dining and gambling, when they decided to go to a brothel. ''Someone invited me along,'' she says, ''but I'd never go that far to be one of the boys.'' It's a story she tells with humor and ease because she has become, if not happy about, at least accustomed to being on the fringes of the male social groups. Even from the fringes she has managed to build good relationships with male colleagues that make her more effective in her job and that make her days easier and more pleasant.

Women on Their Guard

The danger for a woman who makes the discovery that she can't be fully accepted into the boys' club is that she'll become bitter and overly guarded around men. If she does, she only closes off more opportunities for herself and makes men all the more uneasy around her.

Women frequently speak of how painful it is to be left out, to be different, and to be unable to participate—even if the men don't wish to deliberately exclude them. Patricia, a systems analyst for a large engineering company, works almost exclusively with men. She says she never lets her guard down around the men she works with and never feels a part of the group. "I'm definitely not a member in the same way they are," she says. "They're on a softball team and they go out drinking after work and they go to my boss's house at lunchtime to play horseshoes. I have never been invited.

"The chinks in my armor that I might show to a woman I would never show to a man, no matter how well I knew him. I try not to show any of the doubts or uncertainties I feel. In fact, I'm angry if someone before a big presentation or meeting says, 'Aren't you nervous?' It annoys me. I've got my armor up and they've got their armor up too."

Patricia says she doesn't think all women do business with men that way. "But that's how I have to do it," she says. "That's how I keep my ego intact and unbruised. I try not to get involved personally or open up. I don't really trust relationships with men in the business world, because I know there will always be a horseshoe game I won't be invited to and that will hurt."

Although it is understandable that a woman could feel injured and weary from always being the outsider, especially a woman like Patricia who has no female peers at work, she'll cause less wear and tear on her own emotions and do better with men if she avoids throwing up so many barriers around herself. By waiting to be invited to join colleagues in a casual outing, especially lunch, she's looking for a snub where one is probably not intended. No one is in charge of handing out invitations in the office and anyone wanting to join the crowd had better not hang back shyly. Patricia is also confusing personal feelings with business relationships. If friends repeatedly failed to include her in their plans, she would have reason to be hurt. But colleagues are not generally friends. By not attempting to be included in the group she's missing out on opportunities to get to know her boss and colleagues, which might help her do her job better.

The situation looks different from a man's point of view. A man who teaches in the business school of a university says that the only two women on the faculty never hang around the lounge and "gossip with the guys" or go to lunch with everyone. "They're pretty much loners," he says. "They never try to join in." Has he ever invited either to lunch? Well, no; it never occurred to him to do so.

Making It without the Old Boys

Whatever efforts a woman makes, the social contact women have with the men they work with may be less frequent and less informal than what the men share. The problem is partly lack of opportunity—a woman is simply less likely to play golf or be hanging around the locker room where the men are discussing Sunday football. The awkwardness and inappropriateness intrinsic to many male/female get-togethers also hinders women's full participation with men. Many women may not be free in some companies to suggest dinner or drinks with colleagues and rarely can comfortably be included on an overnight outing, such as a hunting or fishing trip.

Says Meredith Fernstrom: "You can't really have much in the way of social contact. The most I tend to have with male colleagues is lunch. You can't very well go out for drinks or dinner because that looks like there's more to it than a business relationship. I wouldn't think it appropriate to call up a [male] colleague and say 'Let's play golf this weekend.' For one thing, I don't play golf, but even if I did I wouldn't do it because it would be very strange for me as a woman to try to set that up."

Given the severe limitations on a woman's opportunities for socializing with men, what can a woman do? First, she can take full advantage of whatever occasions she does have for informal contact—lunches, chatting before a meeting starts, company-sponsored social events, small talk on the telephone. Rather than watching what the men do and imitating their behavior, successful women often find they must take their own paths. "A lot of it is how you relate to one another in meetings," says Fernstrom, "which is the normal way people see each other around here, or on the telephone. I try to be very friendly and inject a sense of humor."

Another thing she can do is not overemphasize the importance of socializing with male colleagues. Being plagued by "What am I missing?" will only hamper you. Some women, like Madelyn Jennings of Gannett, are fortunate enough to be accomplished in the sports men play. "I'm a good golfer and a good tennis player and I'm glad of that," she says. "That has helped my career, in terms of men being comfortable with me, but not in other ways." Real business does get done on the golf course, in the country clubs, and university clubs, but, according to Jennings, how much women are impeded by not participating may be less than it's cracked up to be. Being able to join in is an advantage, but not a "must have." It isn't the critical ingredient that will make or break a woman's career.

Participating in sports events, in fact, can present its own set of problems. If you do engage in sports with men, you must be good. Men don't want to give lessons; they want a worthy opponent. Unless a woman can hold her own in a reasonably competitive game she's better off finding something else to do until the men finish. And if you plan to contend, it helps, as Madelyn Jennings says, "to have a little bit of a thick skin." That will get you through the kinds of situations Jennings has faced repeatedly when golfing with men. Last year, for instance, she was playing in Florida on a Saturday morning with three men; as she rounded the ninth hole she was greeted by the club manager who escorted her off the course—women weren't allowed to tee off before noon.

Remember that although social contact can help build useful business relationships, it still is business that's important. You can gain respect and create good feelings by being a valuable colleague, even if you can't play with the guys. "What it finally comes down to is that someone has to do the work," says Meredith Fernstrom. "You have a case when you're doing a good job and you're the best person doing it. There certainly are times when the golfing buddy gets the promotion, because there's a lot of ego tied up in it, and men have a hard time letting down their buddies.

"But the promotions I've had and the advancement has been on the basis of just a lot of hard work and recognition as being a very competent team player."

If a woman complains that she can't get in with the men and stops there, she won't progress. "I feel that way too," says Fernstrom. "I can say any day that I'm not one of the boys, but that doesn't mean I can't get ahead. I have a certain amount of assertiveness and ambition. Maybe I display it in different ways; I don't wear it on my sleeve and make a big deal out of it. But I do seize the opportunity when it comes along to do something bigger or different. I'm doing more to let people know what I've accomplished. I'm also conscious of trying to nurture some of the relationships that I have with male colleagues in what I consider are appropriate ways to do it. I'm not just sitting back throwing up my hands and saying, 'Well, they'll never let me in, so I'm bound to sit on the sidelines for the rest of my life.' "

8 COMPETITION, COOPERATION, AND CONFIDENCE

Men and boys love competition. Little boys compete and compare endlessly. Who can get the highest score? Make up the silliest stories? Go to bed the latest? Be the best, the biggest, the greatest? Their games center on contests. Competition, seeing how they stack up against other little boys, stimulates and excites them. In its purest form, competition is an aggressive act that males find satisfying.

Boys the country over are instilled with the maxims coaches tack up on locker room walls: "Winning isn't everything; it's the only thing"; "When the going gets tough, the tough get going"; "Winners never quit and quitters never win." That competitiveness pervades the thinking of many men, too. Some turn every encounter, in their personal lives and at work, into a contest with a winner and a loser. Despite many recent changes in our concepts of masculinity and the arrival of the much discussed "new man" who understands emotional sensitivity, there's no evidence that men have given up their desire for maintaining that competitive edge. Men continually need to prove to themselves and to others that they have what it takes.

The curious thing about males is that they don't just enjoy a good contest; they *need* ego challenges and competitive situations in order to achieve. Without them, men lose their motivation. One study of college students, for example, found that males did better on a task when watched by a male peer, while observation made no difference in the women's performance. A study of children showed that boys persisted longer at a task when another boy was present, but the same effect just didn't hold for girls. Something goes on with males

123

when they're in the presence of other males that improves their performance and intensifies their desire to achieve.

And it's not just any competition that will do. What they want most is to compete with other males. Researchers Anthony J. Chapman, Jean R. Smith, and Hugh C. Foot, who have conducted a variety of studies of how children use humor, noticed that boys would often compete with one another to be the first to laugh at jokes and even to laugh hardest and longest. In one study they matched boys and girls aged seven and eight in same-sex and opposite-sex pairs and then showed them slides, each depicting a different joke. A big difference turned up in the responsiveness of boys and girls, according to the sex of their companions. Not *once* did a boy laugh more when matched with a girl than when matched with another boy. For the girls, the sex of their playmate made no difference in how much they laughed. In studies where the children were asked to tell their own jokes, the boys who were matched with boys they weren't friends with told twice as many jokes as other pairs of children (boys with friends, girls with friends, and girls with non-friends). Those boys also laughed more at their *own* jokes than at the ones their companions told.

A study of 94,000 young athletes and their parents in Michigan, reported in *Psychology Today*, found a significant obstacle to the introduction of coed sports in the schools: The boys didn't want girls in their games. In the survey, 67 percent of the young male athletes said they didn't want coed competition; the opposition was even greater among the older boys. When Michigan first introduced coed sports, a third of the boys in the basketball program quit.

Why do boys object to having girls in their games? The answer is necessarily complex and difficult to pin down. But perhaps, as the *Psychology Today* report speculates, one reason may be that girls threaten the integrity of the boys' games. When girls play, the level of competitiveness drops, because winning is not as important to girls. A study done by the National Collegiate Athletic Association of ten- to eighteen-year-olds in summer sports camps showed that boys were three times as likely as girls to name winning as their main reason for competing; other choices the campers could select were fair play and group participation. Not many boys found those to be good reasons for competing. Perhaps boys and girls aren't playing the same game. Certainly the cockiness and swagger that boys take to the playing field is seldom present in the girls, who can be downright nonchalant about how the game is proceeding.

Another explanation may be that boys don't want to play with girls because the threat to their egos should they *lose* is too great to risk.

MEN COMPETING WITH WOMEN

Some of the boyhood fears about and hostilities toward competing with the opposite sex carry over into adulthood and the job.

Men are confused about how to compete with women in the business world and that confusion results in paradoxical attitudes and behavior. On one hand, they think they don't have to compete with women because women aren't in their league. They dismiss women. They see other men as their primary rivals. On the other hand, many men have discovered that some women are quite competent, sometimes more so than men. That worries and confuses them. A man thinks: If women are inferior and yet a woman beats me, what does that say about my abilities? Being beaten by a woman can be an acute blow to the male ego.

A young MBA student, Jim, expresses the annoyance and bafflement of men who are outdone by women. In one of his classes the students divided into small groups and created their own businesses with the use of a computer program. To the dismay of the men, the business run by a group of women prospered; the others foundered. Jim says, "The woman who ran that company was real aggressive, and I noticed it turned a lot of the guys off. We made jokes about her behind her back. We called her 'stupid' or 'vicious,' and different epithets." What she had done that he found "aggressive" was to offer to buy the products sold by the men's companies at low prices. "It was crazy," says Jim. "She made ridiculous offers." But later when the men's companies began to sink, they were forced to sell off their goods to her at her even cheaper prices.

"It wouldn't have been as annoying if it had been a man," Jim says. "Men have a lot of pride. That's why I don't play in the softball league. The women can field better than I can, and they can hit the ball and I can't. All I get is, 'Yeah, he does about as well as the women do.' "

Even if a man doesn't have his masculine pride resting on being better than women and even if he does recognize women as deserving opponents, he may still be confused. That's because he may not be sure how to compete with women. Says a male corporate lawyer: "Sure, men enjoy competing with women—as long as the women compete on men's terms." Men don't know what women's terms are, but they're pretty sure the rules are not as good as the ones men contest with. After all, didn't they learn as boys that girls don't have the fire that makes winning so important?

One rule of competition in the corporate world, which men established, is: No holds barred—but keep tactics carefully concealed so no one else, particularly superiors, can discern your activity. When men compete with women they find keeping competitive moves concealed to be more difficult. That is so, in part, because women and the activities surrounding them stand out when women are scarce.

Another problem might be called "the gentleman factor." A man is likely to think, "If I beat her out or lash into her at this meeting or get tough on this issue, will I look like a bully?" It's not a foolish thought. To others—especially other men—he just may end up looking like a bully beating up on someone less capable. When competing with a woman, a man often feels he can't be quite as tough. Says Dorothy Gregg, who has held executive positions with U.S. Steel and Celanese, "Men can carry on their deadly assassinations of one another without anyone thinking twice about it. With a woman, a man is a little more careful in his behavior than he is competing with another man. He has to be more adroit, more subtle. If he's not, he'll be marked as clumsy, as making a clear attack on the woman—and that's a demerit in the game.''

WOMEN COMPETING WITH MEN

Women make two primary mistakes when they try to compete with men. One is the same mistake men make: They fail to see the opposite sex as serious competitors. Perhaps that's because for some women the only meaningful competition they've engaged in before entering business was with other women, for men. Or perhaps some women unconsciously accept the traditional view of the natural order: Men are superior, women subordinate. Those women will let a man surpass them but devote great energy to making sure that other women aren't getting ahead. That kind of thinking leads to wasted time and energy and diverts women from their goals.

Meredith Fernstrom of American Express says that in her experience, women are more competitive against women than against men, all other matters being equal. "They will sit back and let men break through because they think that's expected," she says. "But with women they feel the emotional responses, the jealousies, and the pettiness." The danger in that kind of thinking struck her recently when she read in her university alumni newsletter that since her alma mater went coed fifteen years ago, no woman has held the office of student government president, editor of the newspaper, or any of the other three or four main leadership positions on campus. Fernstrom recalls that when she attended the school (before it went coed), the environment was highly competitive. It was there she learned many leadership skills. Adding men to the mix seems to have cooled the competitive fire in the women.

The second mistake women make is in thinking they know what competition is when they don't. All achievement is not the result of competition. One young lawyer says of herself: "I'm highly competitive. I've been highly competitive since I was a little kid. If there was a prize for being first, I wanted to be first. If there wasn't a prize, I *still* wanted to be first because that's the prize." Then she adds, "I think the person I'm competing with is myself, almost always." Competition is not a contest with yourself. It is an aggressive, sometimes even hostile battle that necessarily involves the defeat of someone else. Males understand that—and thrive on it. Many females don't and their training in school reinforces their misconceptions. Girls may think their academic achievements are competitive, but in fact it's quite possible to get high grades and perform well throughout school life without ever truly competing, without actually having to prevail over another or to *feel* that you are defeating another. That's true far less often in the post-school world.

One result of women's failure to understand the nature of competition is that they can make the wrong judgments about competitive job situations. They can personalize the contest too much, and in doing so they make the contest even more deadly than it already is. If your ideas are assailed at a meeting, for example, or a proposal of yours is rejected and you view that as a personal attack, you'll be disproportionately wounded, will have a false view of your competitors, and may be moved to counterattack in an inappropriate way. One man who recently moved into a position where he supervises a number of high-level women says, "Women go for the jugular. No matter how vicious things get with other men, they still know it's a game. Not women."

No one likes to lose a battle for a promotion or plum assignment, but women seem to take such losses more personally. A woman might think: "That man I'm competing against thinks I shouldn't be here anyway." Or worse, she might interpret the loss of a promotion as a signal that she doesn't have what it takes to be successful. One woman, a research psychologist who works in personnel at an engineering company, says her experience has told her that men are better able to separate their egos and sense of worth from what happens to them on the job. "A lot of women take everything that happens extremely personally as a threat or blow,'' she says. ''I've watched men take some terrible defeats in political battles and survive intact. I've seen women in the same situation be devastated.''

Women who do personalize business competition must learn to adjust their viewpoint. Instead of trying to guess why a decision went against you (Was it the way I handled the Dallas meeting?), try to figure out why the decision went *with* someone else. Was she or he with the company longer or better suited in some way? Was someone else's proposal better timed or prepared? And most important, how can I do better the next time? If you view every bit of competition at work as a personal assault or personal defeat, you won't survive. No one's emotions and ego can take such battering.

What women often fail to understand is that, vicious as men can be in competitive situations, they are often *enjoying* themselves. Because they are not taking their battles personally, they are freer to accept defeat or to go all out to best another. One seasoned magazine editor, a man, is fond of telling stories about his glory days on the staff of a men's magazine, where he and two other young male editors were pitted continually in an extremely competitive environment. The competition was deliberate and pointed; at weekly staff meetings with the male editor-in-chief the three young men were set against one another in a struggle to suggest the best ideas, best writers, most unusual, most outrageous stories. It wasn't enough to come in with a terrific idea — it had to be more terrific than any of the ideas the other guys brought in that week. They all loved it.

Joining the Competition

That situation would be a nightmare for many women, who often prefer to work with colleagues rather than against them. Although women need not necessarily join the most vicious battles going on at work (after all, some of it is just ritualized male-to-male head-butting), women can't permit themselves to be left out altogether. In order to compete with men—and to get them to compete with you—you have to first let them know you're a worthy opponent.

It's no fun competing with someone who's in the B league if you are—or think you are—triple A.

One of the easiest ways to do that is to learn to join the verbal one-upmanship so characteristic of male conversation. Typical male competitive behavior—in talk as well as deed—centers on "Can you top this?" Men give up the physical rough-and-tumble of boy-hood and trade it for verbal roughhousing. A lot of this talk seems silly, but it has its purpose. Men exchange insults and barbs as a way of comparing and differentiating themselves. Ray Siehndel, a lawyer and businessman in Kansas, explains that talk among men —the jokes and the laughing—is also a way of staking out territory. He admits to some weariness at times of the "guys and the guys' egos," because "we're always doing the same BS," but acknowl-edges it as a given in doing business with men. Even when men aren't jockeying for territory, insults and "I'm better than you" talk is a part of normal, everyday conversation for men. One man, for instance, by coincidence met a colleague's father after work one day. The next afternoon he said to his colleague, "Hey, I met your father last night. How did a nice guy like that end up with a son like you?" His co-worker's response was: "Yeah, he told me he ran into some disreputable guy who knew me."

Women can be wary of such banter because a woman's style would be more direct: "I met your father last night—what a nice man he is." It's not difficult to join the male back-and-forth, however, if you remember two principles: Take *nothing* as a personal insult (even if you're certain it was one), and don't withdraw. If you can come back with a line worthy of "Saturday Night Live," great. But don't worry if you can't; most men can't either. The important thing is to keep yourself in the contest by throwing out a sentence to keep the ball in play. Women too often misinterpret competitive joshing and take it as a negative personal message. They feel disliked and that makes everyone involved uncomfortable. Although some of the talk may very well be hostile (men have a lot of aggression to vent), it's not necessarily intended to do any personal damage.

The difficulty for women is that they haven't had a lot of experience dealing with such situations. Little boys grow up with it, little girls don't. In their play, boys routinely insult and taunt one another. When a boy who wears glasses misses a throw, he can be sure he'll hear: "Hey, what's the matter, aren't four eyes enough?" That boy's feelings may well be hurt, but he knows he'll get his chance to zing the other boy—and he'll take it. Girls rarely engage in such direct attacks.

Withdrawal is the worst thing you can do. It is confusing to men, those boys grown-up and sitting in the next office, when an opponent collapses instead of fighting back. And most men have had experience with women who do just that. Says one man: "I like to trade insults with a woman so long as she doesn't take any of it too seriously or try to make too much of the banter. And as long as she can come back with some good ones, too."

One woman remembers her first interview years ago when she was fresh out of college, looking for a job. She was being quizzed by an older, brusque man who ruffled her feathers by asking whether she could spell. "Yes" was her reply, but what she thought was, "Does he think I went to Vassar to learn spelling?" The interview was not going well. Finally, he began to explain to her that he could sometimes be blunt and wasn't averse to cutting loose with some tough language, the implication being: Would this young thing be able to work in that environment? She was annoyed enough by then to shoot back, "I can spell those words, too." She thinks the comeback got her the job.

For a woman in the workplace it's essential to learn that give-and-take, that "chalk one up for me" behavior. If she doesn't show herself to be capable of a little competitive byplay, men will never believe she can compete on the important matters. Ray Siehndel says the women he works with "just aren't involved" in the one-up-manship of the men. "The women never participate," he says. "They aren't on the same plateau with the male competitiveness." Participating in the verbal repartee will help put you on the same plateau—and it may help you *feel* potent when a real power play comes along.

Also helpful is remembering that *weak* men are the ones most threatened by competition with women. A weak man will frequently try to combat a woman by pulling the competition into an area where he is more comfortable and more competent than she—and that's in the male culture. Such a man might, for example, make a point of turning conversation to small talk that deliberately excludes the woman. Consultant Denise Cavanaugh says men particularly love to share "road stories"—what happened to them one winter in Detroit or in the train station in Philly when they were traveling for the company. She advises women to participate and trade stories too—but suggests a woman avoid topping the stories, particularly if she thinks the man is doing it because he's uncomfortable with her presence.

Although it's important for women to get into the contest with men, being on the outside isn't always a disadvantage. If a woman can swallow the insult of not being taken seriously by men, she can use their attitude to her advantage. One woman, early in her career in the construction business, was able to get valuable information from potential competitors because none of them—all males— believed this young woman trying to put together a general contracting firm could ever be a threat. She's now head of a multimillion- dollar commercial construction company—and finds she no longer can get insider information free.

The Cooperative Element

Although women certainly aren't unable to compete, they are very good at cooperating and collaborating. Given a choice they prefer sharing rather than seizing, smoothing rather than confronting. And those can be valuable traits in the work world, highly regarded by men and women. One man who works for a woman says he admires the way his boss can appear helpful and cooperative and still "tell people to go to hell." If someone asks her to do something not in her realm or wants to impose on the people who work for her, she can write a gracious, polite memo that makes her seem helpful and yet still enables her to get her way. "She turns things around so that they are *handled*," he says. "I'm not good at that. I break eggs."

Both sexes have the capacity for cooperative and competitive behavior, but in different proportions: Men are more competitive, women more cooperative. According to psychologist Jean Baker Miller, cooperation is not as appealing to males because they perceive it as losing something or giving something away. Men think they must be independent, go it alone, *win*, or they haven't succeeded. Just as women often misconstrue competition, men don't understand cooperation. Few men realize that it isn't altruism—it is behavior that aids others while at the same time benefiting oneself.

Women are quick to learn that letting others gain points is one way of getting some themselves. Laura, an MBA at a large company, works for a woman, Frances, who is one of the few in the company to have made it to the level of vice president. "She is a great manipulator of people—in a positive sense—and she's gotten things out of men in situations where men would compete for a piece of the action." Frances tries to get what she wants without going head-to-head with men. She's also willing to lose a battle now and then. A year ago Laura was working on an important piece of business. A young man who was moving rapidly in the company worked in an area that overlapped Laura's. During the dividing-up-the-turf conversation, Frances permitted him to take away Laura's project.

Later she explained to Laura that the reason she gave up the work was that this fellow was a strong up-and-comer; resisting him now could only mean trouble for Laura and Frances later, so why not make a friend instead? Laura wonders whether the pleasure in doing that work would have outweighed making someone angry, but she thinks her boss was probably right, considering the type of company they work for. "It's a young, fast-paced, high-growth company where people are touched by the magic wand and zoom up to the president's suite," says Laura. "It's dangerous to make enemies of someone who's sitting in the next office; he may be five steps ahead of you tomorrow."

Competition and cooperation are not opposite sides of the same coin. They are qualities and skills that frequently are needed at the same time. Much work-related competition, like sports competition, relies on cooperation within the team in order to defeat other groups.

Women are generally better off trying to gain the cooperation of men than trying to fight head-to-head with them; arousing male aggression can lead to alienation for a woman and doesn't necessarily get her what she wants. Another female executive in Laura's company is not as adept as Frances in finding alternatives to the contest of "who gets it." The other woman tries to "beat the guys at their own game," says Laura. She fails to control and direct her own aggression. "She walks into someone's office and says, 'Goddamn it, the XYZ deal is mine and *you can't have it.*'" That woman is successful—she's a vice president—but she's universally deemed unlikely to make it to the inner circle of top management. She's so good at what she does that her bosses have been unable to resist promoting her thus far. But her belligerence is about to get in the way. Unless a woman can sustain a tough manner indefinitely—and be right most of the time—she's at continual risk of falling on her face. Working cooperatively and building allies is a better approach.

A MATTER OF CONFIDENCE

Competing—and losing—are both much easier if you possess a heavy dose of confidence. It seems, however, that when the self-assurance is passed around, males get the bulk of it. Even in grade school years, boys have a sense of personal strength and potency that's clearly stronger than girls'. When it comes to assessing their own abilities and power, males generally take the assertive approach and look on the positive side. Both sexes tend to err in their self-evaluations: men on the side of overestimating their performance and women in underestimating theirs.

A summary of research on how males and females score in predicting their success at tasks, reported by psychologists Jacklin and Maccoby in *The Psychology of Sex Differences*, shows that in *all* studies there is either no difference in how the sexes rate themselves or males showed more confidence. Females never, in a wide range of studies examined in the research, scored higher than males. College women, for instance, when asked what grades they think they'll get in the next grading period, are likely to predict they'll do less well than their past performance would indicate; males, on the other hand, predict they'll do at least as well, perhaps better than they've been doing. One study of boys showed they were unlikely even to hear negative feedback about their performances. When told they were insensitive, boys didn't change their self-ratings on sensitivity. Boys are also more likely to defend their egos by turning against whatever is blocking their way; girls are more likely to blame themselves, which never helps build anyone's self-confidence.

In studies of males and females holding first-level management positions, psychologist Kay Deaux of Purdue University found that males evaluated their job performance more favorably and rated themselves as having more ability and greater intelligence than women did. In one of Deaux's studies, the men not only saw themselves as performing significantly better overall than did the women, but they viewed their jobs as being more difficult.

Deaux's studies also show that men tend to cite ability as accounting for their success and tend to deny responsibility for their failures. Women use fewer internal reasons, such as skill, to explain their successes and tend to use more temporary explanations, such as luck. Those differences have important implications and influence on future behavior. It's plain to see that if you think you performed well because the wind was right, rather than because you're good at what you do, you're not going to approach the same task with confidence the next time out.

Even a woman who doesn't necessarily lack confidence can appear to in contrast to the occasional flagrant displays of ambition and assurance from men. One woman tells the story of a female boss in her company who interviewed a young man just out of Harvard and turned him down for the job. Instead of going on to the next corporation, smarting over the rejection, the young man called someone else at the company and said, "Look, I just had an interview that I don't think fairly reflected my abilities. I'd like to see someone else." Not only did he get another interview, he got the job, and within a short time he moved ahead of the woman who had originally turned him down.

Another woman says she thinks the men in her company "float to the top" because they expect to. "They don't like being low-paid and they don't like being put in the position of being secondary," she says. "Men have been led to believe that they don't have to accept second place, so they find a way to get around it."

Those displays of confidence and competence are part of the assertive strategy that males use to present themselves to others. Males prefer to appear powerful and competent; they minimize any deficiencies. They like to assert status and in doing so to establish distance between themselves and others.

Females are less likely to choose that strategy. They prefer to neutralize status and present themselves as more typical in performance. Their intentions are affiliative; they establish links with others rather than create distance. The trouble with the female approach at work, however, is that presenting yourself as average, minimizing your strengths, and blaming yourself for every failure is as good as being—and feeling—mediocre. In the male world, you're expected to boast a bit and exaggerate performances. And women need to learn how to do that, too.

In a survey conducted by the search firm Korn/Ferry International, 11 percent of the senior executive women listed lack of confidence as a barrier to their success. It was second only to "being a woman" as the most often noted obstacle. Little wonder that confidence can falter in the upper ranks, however, where women are highly scrutinized and subjected to a different standard from men.

The double standard women are subjected to goes back to the old notion that the natural order is dominant men, subordinate women. If a woman wants to move ahead, she must prove she's an exception.

"At higher levels," says Meredith Fernstrom, "men are just not used to having a woman be part of the team. Because of that, you're a lot more visible and a lot more vulnerable as far as what you're expected to do and the scrutiny that's placed on you."

That scrutiny and double standard can lead a woman at any level to be less sure of her skills and more fearful of making a mistake.

HOW MANY MISTAKES CAN YOU MAKE?

Everyone makes mistakes. Men, however, don't seem to agonize over them the way women tend to. The reason may be in part that men are both permitted more mistakes and penalized less for each in the workplace than women are. But men also seem to understand which mistakes don't count as much. Women strive to overachieve; they perceive every setback as major. "They go out to win every skirmish," says Vivian Manuel, head of a public relations firm, "when what they really need to win is the war." In Manuel's experience with women who have worked for her in her business and in the corporate jobs she's held, women seem not to understand that mistakes are expected. "You have to be right 51 percent of the time—but it has to be the right 51 percent," she says. "Typos in annual reports and quarterlies and employee newspapers are embarrassing, but if the typo is in the chairman's name *that's* a serious mistake."

One reason women have difficulty putting their mistakes in perspective is that they often are detail oriented. An overconcern with detail often reflects the cautious, earnest way women approach work. One woman explains her careful, thorough methods this way: "Something goes on in my mind that says, 'Think about the consequences; really roll this thing out to all the names and faces in front of you.' That thinking sometimes holds up a project and makes it an hour or two hours late while I get approvals or feel people out, but I find myself doing that more. And I find the women I work with doing it more." She says the men she works with aren't "so sensitive to the company's needs" or to the "thorough way to do the job." "And yet," she says, "I don't see it damaging them. I don't know if I'm being thorough because I feel concerned about the consequences of not checking everything out a million times or because it's my habit. Maybe men don't do it because they don't care what the consequences are—and they are *allowed* not to care. With the men, all that matters is doing the deal. 'Did you do the deal?' 'Yeah I did the deal.' That's all you hear. And it's deals that earn you another stripe."

The thoroughness and perfectionism that woman describes can come off to men as insecurity and lack of confidence. Ray Siehndel says that he finds women are sometimes too cautious in negotiations. That signals to him a fear of making a decision. "Women have a tendency," he says, "to take a position and freeze it until they've had time to do more research—or something. I don't deal that way. I go in ready to compromise, ready to deal and move. And I find a lot of women will just freeze up: 'That is it, take it or get out of here.' " He sees that behavior not as toughness, but as fear. "They just aren't secure in their own ability. I think most of the women I deal with are probably better prepared than I am and smarter than I am. I don't think that's the problem. It's a question of insecurity, being afraid to make a mistake."

The fear of making mistakes holds women back not only in individual negotiations, but also in their career movement. Meredith Fernstrom at American Express says she sees a lot of women who are reluctant to push themselves ahead. "They feel competent in what they're doing but often don't want to expand their horizons and take on something bigger," she says. "I was talking to one of our foreign managers in Germany who was telling me that some of his women are far and away his best staff people. He offered one of them a promotion to take on a bigger managerial role, but she didn't want it. He had to practically talk her into it.

"It's that attitude of: 'Gee, I'm here and I know I can do this and do it well and I'd be perfectly happy to sit here and do it for x number of years.' And yet I would guarantee you that if she had done that, and a man who was less qualified had been promoted, she would have resented it like crazy.

"It's on both sides; men have to be willing to give women the *opportunity* to fail or succeed equally, because that's how you grow. Women at the same time have to be willing to take those risks and know that they can grow into them.

"I think every job I've had in the last three or four positions, I went into with a certain amount of apprehension about how I would perform. It was always either a new position where there was no frame of reference and I had to come in and create it from scratch, or it was a larger area of responsibility beyond what I'd had previous experience with. And yet I think what management is telling you is: 'Hey, you've done well at this level and we have confidence that you can do it at the next level.' That in turn has to give you a certain amount of confidence."

WORK LIKE HELL AND ADVERTISE

Feeling confident isn't enough, however. You have to project confidence also. Men know that a sure way to unsteady your opponent is to talk big and boast about your expectations of success. You can't sit back and wait to be noticed and rewarded. For women, whose inclinations are affiliative, self-promotion doesn't always come easy. Meredith Fernstrom says she has had to teach herself to blow her own horn, a trait she doesn't come by naturally. She's guided by what she once heard a company president say to explain his success: "Early to bed, early to rise, work like hell and advertise." It's not enough to do a good job; people have to know you're doing it.

Fernstrom, one of the few women in the country who holds a top-level executive position in a *Fortune* 100 firm, says, "I've found I've had to be a little more vocal than is normally my style. Especially in a company like this, where it's very competitive and very market-intensive. You've got to be the best and the first. There's a value placed on people who are not only doing a good job, but letting the right people know in the right way. So I do things like circulate memos to people who I think should be aware of some of the things I'm doing. Nothing frivolous or things I don't think are important." She says that a few years ago she might have just sent a memo to her boss with the assumption that if he thought it was good enough he'd send it on. Now, with her boss's consent, she sends memos to the chairman or vice-chairman or heads of subsidiary companies. "Just trying to let them know more about the kinds of things I'm doing," she says.

It's important to remember too that many successful people have come back from failures to build impressive careers. Madelyn Jennings says that one of the favorite Gannett stories is about chairman Al Neuharth's first venture out of college. It was a tabloid in South Dakota called *SoDak Sports*, which he started with a borrowed $25,000. When it folded soon thereafter, he was left penniless and owing. "Many people think," says Madelyn, "that one of the reasons Al is so driven to do things well and be successful and make a name for himself is because he started off with a failure." Who knows, had he succeeded he might still be running the *SoDak Sports*—instead of a multimillion-dollar communications company.

9 SEX IN THE OFFICE

Whether you find the chemistry between men and women valuable or an annoyance you'd like to banish from the work world, doesn't matter. In either case, it's here to stay. Anthropologist David Givens reminds us that all mating animals have to be able to distinguish between the sexes—and if they can't they're in trouble.

"Androgyny as a principle doesn't work for our species very well," says Givens. "We are a little more androgynous than some of the other primates, but not a lot. There is always going to be that attraction across the sexes." Our ability to make distinctions between the sexes and our attraction to the opposite one aren't traits we can leave behind when we head off to work.

"Business is not as logical as they might teach you in business school," says Givens. "It's one of the most personal arenas. There's no way to weed out personal characteristics." And sex is perhaps the most important of personal characteristics. Even though sex may have nothing to do with the job or task at hand, it is far from irrelevant to the workplace.

The first thing each of us notices about another person is her or his sex. And that's just as true in business as in social situations. Most of us wouldn't want it any other way. In fact, anyone whose sex is doubtful isn't going to fare well at work. And anyone who can't respond to the opposite sex probably won't do well either. The "quasi-courting" nonverbal behavior discussed in Chapter 3 is a basic interaction between the sexes. Most people are accustomed to using sexual signals, often unconsciously, to create a feeling of intimacy and understanding. Psychiatrist Albert Scheflen, who first

141

described the behavior, observed that some people are unable to quasi-court; instead they freeze or withdraw and end up alienating others. He said that in most groups such people, "like the overcautious driver, have a provocative and disruptive effect, while they appear to be models of decorum and cooperativeness." In other words, people who are completely sexless and unable to relate to others on the subtlest of sexual levels strike the rest of us as, at best, odd.

To be effective on the job, a woman has to know a great deal about how her sexual attractiveness affects her work and the men she works with. She must take care regarding the sexual signals she sends to men, and she must be expert at knowing what the signals men send really mean.

MEN SEE SEX WHERE IT ISN'T

Women are closely linked with sexuality in the minds of men. They are so accustomed to seeing women as sexual beings—not just lovers and wives, but also mothers, whose sex is critical to identity—that they see sex everywhere in their dealings with women. Men are so attuned to sexual cues that they sometimes pick up signals that weren't sent. Women's suspicions that men often impute sexual interest to female behavior when it's not intended have recently been confirmed. In a study conducted by Antonia Abbey at Northwestern University, men and women were paired and instructed to have a conversation. The men tended to see the women, whom they had just met, as being seductive, while the women saw themselves as just friendly. The males also were more sexually attracted to the females than the females were to them, and the men were more likely to rate themselves as flirtatious and seductive.

Although this study was done with college students, who might be expected to have their sexual antennae well tuned, working women encounter the same types of misunderstandings. If, for instance, a woman tries to be part of the group at work and goes out for a drink with the men, she'll probably be doing it because she wants to send a message like this: "I want to be on the team; I want to feel relaxed and I want to belong; I want to be able to give you a hug when we win a big one. That's how I am and how I relate to people." Some men won't hear that message. Instead they will think she's attracted to them or is "available." (If she's not available, then why isn't she home with her family? What could going out and drinking with the boys mean except that she's "looking"?)

Sometimes men misinterpret women's behavior quite mistakenly; simply from *habit* they expect women to be sexual. Michael Korda, author of *Power! How to Get It, How to Use It*, says that men expect women to use sex as a weapon. "It's part of their ingrained distrust of women in general," he writes. Some men like to imagine women are sexually aggressive because such behavior flatters men and puts women in a familiar role. Those men are likely to interpret all sorts of signals as sexual. Even when a woman uses body language to signal dominance by standing close, staring, or touching, some men will see that as sexual. Men just as often, however, deliberately misinterpret a woman's behavior.

SEX AND POWER

When a man brings sex into business—whether it's in the form of a blatant invitation for sex, an off-color joke, or any of the myriad means men have for reminding women of their sexuality—the issue involved is not necessarily sexual attraction. He is very likely using sex to assert his power over a woman. Jealousy, hostility, and fear can motivate men to use sex as a put-down.

Men confuse sex and power. For them, sex is just one of the many ways they have of exerting their authority. Because sex and power are often confused in men's minds and behavior, the work environment can be tricky for women. Power assertion from men can easily be disguised as gentlemanly behavior. A compliment on a woman's appearance, a fatherly pat, or a jovial "You're the best-looking sales rep in four states," can have the appearance of kindliness and simple friendliness. Yet it may leave a woman feeling distinctly uncomfortable, because such seemingly trivial incidents are ways men have of reminding themselves—and women—of male dominance.

Any woman who works with men must be vigilant; she must know when a man is using sex as a means of control and not fall into the trap of feeling flattered or insulted by sexual attention. What a woman must do instead is recognize when sex is being used as a power play—and respond accordingly.

Common techniques employed by men are to comment on women's attractiveness or refer to them with endearments ("honey," "sweetheart") in front of male colleagues. Whether a man does that deliberately or not, it gets the other men to focus on the woman's sexuality rather than her professionalism. Such behavior undermines her power and authority, though it often comes in the guise of gracious behavior. A man might, for example, put his arm around a woman to usher her into a meeting. By doing so, he puts himself in a protective role and diminishes her—ever so subtly—in the eyes of other men.

Your response to such a ploy must be equally gracious. You'll do yourself no good to snub him for being what is to him and all the men present merely polite. Accept his gesture, but as soon as possible do something that will assert your authority. You might, for instance, immediately use a similar gesture on him, such as inviting him to sit or even pulling out his chair for him. (If the man in question is much more powerful than you, you'll do better to select one of the other men for your power gestures; you'll gain the same effect without threatening a higher-up.) Other tactics might include asking one of the men to assist you in your presentation at the meeting, or you can pull the conversation to some topic that gives you status (a project you're in charge of, for instance). Your objective is to remind the men promptly that you are a colleague as well as a woman.

When men use sexual power plays during actual business dealings, the intent is usually malicious—and the effect more serious. One woman remembers making a strong point at a seminar that was dominated by men. The men had been hostile and had deliberately excluded her from the proceedings whenever possible. When she won her point, one of the men said, "Well, guys, she's a great date, anyway." The unspoken second half of that sentence was: "even though she's a bitch here." (The woman had never dated that man or any present.) His comment, said in jest and seeming on the surface to be complimentary, degraded the point she was making and deflected attention from her competence to her sexuality. The temptation might have been to come back with a cutting remark like, "How would you know, my dear?" Men are so sensitive about their sexual powers, however, that women are better off not threatening them, especially in front of other men. In a circumstance like that, the best a woman can do is either come back with a joke that reminds the men of her competence (something like, "Well, I've got brains and good looks, now all I need is wealth"). Her other option is to ignore the comment and reassert her point.

A man is likely to draw attention to a woman's sex when he's insecure about competing with her. If a man and a woman were working together to divide up a budget, for example, and he began to fear she was gaining points, he might start joking around and say something like, "Marion, it sure would be easier to negotiate with you if you didn't wear blouses like that one." The remark would probably distract and disarm her, and he would have successfully pulled the competition into an area where he was comfortable and where he had more power. If a man is having trouble topping a woman, sex is always a handy weapon. Korda says that men who are experienced power players "can easily put down a woman and flatter her at the same time." Flirtation, flattery, seduction, and innuendo, he says, "all can be turned into a technique of control."

Men especially like to turn business relationships with women into more familiar and comfortable social male/female relationships. All the traditional male roles—father, husband, lover—are useful to men in the workplace because they help men control women. Men flirt with their subordinates, for example, to make it difficult for them to ask for raises or to protest work that's outside their job descriptions. Being fatherly permits men to assert parental authority over women.

One of the strongest weapons a man can use against a woman is to circulate rumors that she is sleeping with powerful men. If people believe it (whether it's true or not), it undermines her credibility as almost nothing else can. The implication is that the only way she can accomplish anything significant is if men grant it to her.

Weak and insecure men are the ones most likely to bring out the heavy artillery in the sexual realm. They use sexual assertion over women because they don't have any other way of exerting power—and it is critical to a man's self-esteem that he be able to exert power of some sort. If a man can't use or doesn't have a lot of power he'll use sexual assertion. That's one reason sexual harassment of women is more prevalent at lower levels. As soon as a man gets some political power in his job, he's less likely to need to use sexual power over women. The more powerful a woman is, on the other hand, the more difficult it will be for a man to use sex to put her down. Says one high-ranking woman: "It takes a very insecure man to try to put me down sexually—and it just doesn't work."

Big Daddies, Sexist Pigs, and Wolves

The blatant types are usually the easiest to deal with. If a man is being truly obnoxious, it will be obvious to others as well and you probably won't need to do anything except ignore him. One woman who has had her share of louts pressing close and making lewd remarks in business situations says, "Often the best response is no response. If you try to make a smart remark every time someone makes a sexual comment, you'll find them doing it even more. Worse is falling into the trap of helping him out by making it funny. It's not funny, it's dumb. How do you respond to something that's dumb? You ignore it."

For the really piggish men, those who can only see women as sexual beings in relationship to men, labeling yourself as taken can be the simplest and least painful way to stop their behavior. Men who are hard-core sexists have no respect for a woman's wishes, but often will respect another man's territory. One woman who works in the computer industry says she has encountered countless men who simply don't know how to behave around her. One married man made frequent sexual advances toward her and even arrived on her doorstep one morning with breakfast. She found that a useful technique for discouraging him was to talk about her husband. She has even alluded to having a *jealous* husband. Although in about 99 percent of work situations, hiding behind a jealous husband amounts to political suicide, it can be useful in extreme circumstances. When faced with the behavior of pigs and wolves, remember that your objective is to stop the behavior, particularly around others. Your mission is not to teach him a lesson or to get even.

Look for allies in men as well. Many working men, whether or not they are sensitive to the *reasons* sexual references are offensive to women, will find risqué comments and sexual innuendo out of place in the office. Align yourself with those men. If nothing else, they will also find the behavior of the pigs and wolves impolite and in poor taste.

Occasionally, you'll encounter men who might be called likable sexists. They are generally reasonable and pleasant in their behavior, but sometimes go overboard around women. Depending on his personality and yours, handle the situation by either gently embarrassing him with humor (mock his comments, showing him how his words sound to you) or by taking him aside and telling him that you want a business relationship, not a personal one. The straightforward approach is often the best—the more women speak up about what bothers them, the better. The trick is to be friendly, not confrontational. Remember again that your objective is to get him to stop the behavior; accusing him of evil motives will get you nowhere. If a colleague calls you "Sugar," for instance, and you'd just as soon be addressed by your name, say something to him *privately* like, "I know it's just your manner and you mean well, but I'd much rather

you called me by my name. 'Sugar' sounds belittling, even though
you don't mean it that way.''

A 1981 survey of readers of the *Harvard Business Review* indicated
that a large number of men are simply ignorant of the effects of
sexual comments. They don't know what's offensive to women or
why, and they expect women to tell them when a remark is not
appreciated. Sometimes you'll have to do just that.

Traveling, especially to trade shows and sales meetings, will likely
bring you into contact with conventioneers, a special kind of sexist
who often doesn't show his colors until he gets on the road. Conventions pose problems for women because, as one marketing representative says, ''Men put all their controls aside in such situations.
They haven't lost control. They've just decided not to be in control.''
Sometimes convention settings encourage outrageous behavior from
men and make doing business difficult for women. In such locations,
sexual innuendo is pervasive. A man can't turn his head in the hotel
without being reminded of sex. Women who are dressed to be noticed
are everywhere, making it difficult for businesswomen. In such situations a woman can expect all the usual convention jokes (''Hey,
I heard there aren't enough hotel rooms; we'll have to double up'').

One woman was standing in line waiting to check into a hotel in
Las Vegas for a convention when the man in line in front of her
began flirting. He told her how lucky her company was to have
someone as ''cute'' as she working for them and persisted in his
attentions. ''It was very uncomfortable,'' she says. ''On one hand,
I didn't want to offend him—I didn't know who he was, and he
might have been a client. And because it was a public setting I felt
safe. His remarks were in poor taste but they weren't dangerous. I
don't think that just because someone is rude enough to embarrass
me that I should be rude, too. I just backed away and through my
tone of voice let him know I wasn't interested. He eventually left
me alone.''

In such circumstances a businesswoman must remember that, despite the party mood, she is still conducting business. Such meetings

are not the time to bring out your sexiest dinner dress, even if dressy clothes are called for, or to let down your hair. Don't flirt, don't let yourself get into compromising situations, and don't drink any more than you would at a business lunch.

The last type of troublemaker you're likely to encounter is the older man who turns into a fool around younger women (to him, any woman under fifty seems young). He can't pass you without commenting on your good looks or youth. He finds excuses to hug and kiss. For the most part, such men have little power; their behavior comes from confusion over seeing women in positions of authority; they have no idea how to relate to a female business colleague. Such men are annoying, but generally harmless. Don't worry about them. Use your energy to combat the tactics of more powerful and subtle men.

Friendly Flirting

Sexual incidents, used against women, can be treacherous. They can seriously subvert a woman's effectiveness on the job. And while at times you might prefer to banish sex from work, it can't be done. Women who try to banish sex—or worse, be sexless themselves—seldom succeed. The solution for women is not to deny their sexuality or femininity, but to control it and to keep men from using sex to denigrate them.

It doesn't help to get so fearful of the sex and power issue that you can't relax and enjoy men. You'll make a serious mistake if you punish all men for the behavior of the boors. Women and men who are equals and who respect one another can enjoy doing business together—and can even enjoy a little flirting. The sexual tension that exists between women and men doesn't get in the way as long as respect, a sense of humor, and an easy comfort level also exist. One woman says she finds that one man she works with can throw his arm around her in a friendly way one minute and the next they can discuss a tough issue. Their pleasure in one another, which is purely friendship, doesn't get in the way of business because sex is not being used to exploit anyone.

Women sometimes make the mistake of overreacting to men's behavior. One young woman worked in construction with "a bunch of young, enlightened guys" who welcomed her and even treated her as their "cause"; they liked having a woman on the job and wanted her to do well. But she had trouble dealing with one who wanted to flirt with her. She overreacted by backing away severely and being cold to him. As a result, she alienated all the men.

A better way to handle that situation might have been to take the one who wanted to flirt aside and say something direct, like: "Look, I seem to be getting these signals from you and can't quite figure out whether you mean them or not. I really want to be your colleague, but I'm choosing not to get involved with any of the men I work with." His reply could be, "I want to be a friend, too, and didn't mean to indicate more." In that case, she could say, "Great, I'm sorry I misread you." Or instead he might say, "Yeah, I was interested in getting something going." If that happened she could restate her point, taking care not to offend or appear to reject him. By being direct and calm, she avoids escalating the situation.

Another young woman says she was so fearful of men treating her as a woman, instead of as a colleague, that she was overly conservative with her dress and manner. She wore rigid business suits every day and never left her office to visit another office without a pad and pen in hand. With the encouragement of an older female colleague she has begun to relax her style. She dresses in a more feminine way and lets herself get comfortable when she goes into male colleagues' offices for informal meetings. Now that she's not trying to hide being a woman, she's more relaxed in all her dealings with men. "I even kick off my shoes and put my feet on a table," she says.

A very fine line separates using your sexuality to manipulate men and simply permitting yourself to be a woman. Advertising agency owner Daniela Kuper has found that she sometimes needs to "calm down" her femininity around men in business, but that she doesn't try to deny it. She acknowledges, in fact, that her ability to get along with men has been an advantage to her. She worked for a man once who taught her a great deal about the advertising business; the two worked well together and Kuper says that part of their success was based on the man/woman energy between them.

"We had a lot of good chemistry between us," she says. "If I had been a fat slob I probably would have had to grovel my way on my own. But there was this wonderful dynamism between us that kept his interest level up and made him give me a lot more. He was very accessible to me. He took me everywhere. I went to every meeting and watched everything. I learned right out in the field."

Kuper also warns that "too much looseness and familiarity before its proper time tends to cut into your validity." Kuper is a woman who enjoys men and has always gotten along well with them. But she has had to learn to balance her behavior at work, particularly now that she owns her own business. There's always a certain amount of tension between men and women, she says, and if a woman leans too much one way she becomes bitchy and cold, too much the other way and she loses her authority. "I'm very careful about how I project myself with men," she says.

Women who have a tendency to be flirtatious and to have fun with men are in deep trouble if that's the only way they can behave around men. But women who are afraid of the man/woman chemistry are boring and stiff. Wearing severe suits, talking tough, and rejecting every smile or hint of friendliness from men is no more a sensible way for a woman to behave on the job than is playing the vamp.

"The best ground to be on," says Kuper, "is warm human-being ground. You almost can't go wrong if you're being open and warm and haven't puppeted yourself to a personality that's not yours, if you're not going so far as to be coy or coquettish, but you're not being mechanical either."

A Team, Not a Couple

A particular danger for a woman working with one man is that the two may be seen not as colleagues but as a couple. In even the most innocent situations, when no sexual meaning is intended by anyone involved, sex can be called into play. That's because a man and a woman, particularly if they are close in age, look like a couple to the world.

Being mistaken for lovers instead of colleagues is as embarrassing to men as it is to women. One man tells about going to lunch with his boss, a woman, when they happened to select the same meal. The waitress, after taking their orders, asked whether the two had been married long, and did they often order the same thing? Neither the man nor his boss said anything to make light of the situation—both were so surprised by the remark. In such a situation, the glimpse of yourself as others see you throws the relationship into momentary confusion. Imagining himself, even for a moment, married to his boss—along with all the sexual and other implications—embarrassed and befuddled the man so much that he couldn't make a joke of it. The two let it drop.

There's nothing either could have done in that situation to prevent the waitress from mistaking them for a couple, and the damage was minimal. More dangerous than being mistaken by a stranger, of course, is giving your colleagues the impression, even inadvertently, that you and a male co-worker have something other than a business relationship. That will cause tensions and jealousies. Women have to make a strong effort to reassure colleagues that there is not a sexual basis for their relationships to male bosses and co-workers. One woman says that she had an especially close relationship with a male boss that resulted in much bitterness from her male peers. One of those men was so upset by it that he quit talking to the woman. They worked together in the same small office, but he managed to avoid speaking to her for almost a year.

In order to avoid the appearance of being one half of a couple, a woman may have to monitor her behavior more carefully than a man does. For example, a top executive might take on a young male up-and-comer in the company and give him special privileges—riding in the company limo, access to high-level meetings, lunching with important clients—all to groom him for promotion. Such special treatment is likely to cause others to resent the young man, but he will clearly be seen as more powerful and influential than his peers. A woman in the same situation, however, risks being mistaken first for a secretary or assistant (others will be unsure whether she's in those meetings to take notes or to learn) and, second, she risks the appearance that she's getting special attention in exchange for sexual favors. The solution is not to avoid such situations—they are treasured opportunities for advancement—but to work extra hard to keep up a professional image. She must, for instance, avoid any suggestion that she knows personal details about the life of the executive.

SEXUAL JOKING

Women may at times be successful in keeping men from misinterpreting their behavior as sexual and from using sex as a power tool. But women can't keep men from making sexual jokes. Men use sexual jokes for two reasons: to promote male bonding, and to express and release sexual desires and hostilities. Not all men have such needs, but many do.

Sexual humor used by men to create a group feeling is often characterized by banter and boyish elbow-ribbing. Because sexual joking is usually directed toward women and excludes women, it gives men a sense of closeness with one another. A woman who works in personnel in an almost all-male industry says she sees much of this sort of behavior among the men she works with; they will, for instance, interrupt a business meeting to point out an attractive young woman passing by. She once attended a hockey game with a small group of male colleagues and they got so involved with one another they forgot she was there. "I watched them doing their businessman-turned-sixteen-ogling-the-girls routine," she says. "They teased one another about their sex lives—and lack of sex lives. I just ignored it." There was nothing sexual about the men's behavior. In adolescent boys it's called "homosocial" behavior; it's quasi-sexual behavior solely for the purpose of developing a relationship with another male. It develops camaraderie, a feeling of group, of common maleness. Women are irrelevant.

The authors of *Why Can't Men Open Up?*, Steven Naifeh and Gregory White Smith, write: "Tales of sexual adventures, innuendoes of inadequacy, paeans to the female anatomy, and off-color jokes are usually nothing more than a filler: harmless banter to keep the conversation going, to maintain the lines of communication with other men. . . . Sex talk is for many men what small talk is for many women: a form of caring."

Women usually know—often intuitively—when men are using humor in the buddy-building way and it's rarely offensive. A woman may feel excluded, but not insulted. If that were the only kind of sexual joking that went on between men, women would probably think little of it. But it's not. Some men also engage in hostile, aggressive sexual humor that is clearly directed against women, and that is something women seldom find funny.

According to Freud, hostile and obscene jokes permit people to explore and express feelings that society tells us we shouldn't. Obscene joking is generally male behavior; it is a substitute for seduction. A woman's role in such humor is to be the object and impetus. Freud explains that obscene jokes "make possible the satisfaction of an instinct (whether lustful or hostile) in the face of an obstacle . . . [which] is in reality nothing other than women's incapacity to tolerate undisguised sexuality . . ." Woman's resistance, he said, is essential to the joke; it heightens the hostility and titillation.

"If a man in a company of men enjoys telling or listening to smut," Freud writes, "the original situation [i.e., seduction], which owing to social inhibitions cannot be realized, is at the same time imagined. A person who laughs at smut . . . is laughing as though he were the spectator of an act of sexual aggression. . . . Smut is like an exposure of the sexually different person to whom it is directed. By the utterance of the obscene words it compels the person who is assailed to imagine the part of the body or the procedure in question and shows her that the assailant is himself imagining it. It cannot be doubted that the desire to see what is sexual exposed is the original motive of smut." Little wonder such humor can cause women extreme discomfort.

Most of us live and work in reasonably polite society where obscenity—even when couched in humor—is not tolerated. And many men today have had their consciousness of women's rights raised at least to the point where they know there's something wrong with sexual joking around women. They may not know what, but they are wary enough and unsure enough about how a woman will react that they usually will refrain from telling their raunchiest stories in the presence of women.

In an essay about male humor, science fiction writer Isaac Asimov explained that one of the reasons men enjoy all-male groups is that they can tell "off-color jokes." Those jokes, he writes, which usually make women the butts and victims, serve a useful psychological function: They help relieve the tensions men feel from the lifelong domination of women. Asimov claims he doesn't like male chauvinism, but also doesn't think we should suppress the jokes that are useful to men. "I would, instead," he writes, "prefer to invite women into the charmed circle and have them tell their jokes, too, which perhaps will help remove some of *their* hang-ups." The trouble is, he writes, women protest that they can't tell jokes because they can't remember them. "They're just defaulting on their responsibilities," he writes, "and, as long as they do, they encourage us men to put our heads together and tell our chauvinist jokes after a nervous glance hither and thither assures us that no woman can hear us."

Of course, Asimov is writing with a certain amount of wryness —enough to protect himself behind humor should anyone criticize his point of view. But his suggestion that women join in the fun is hollow. Not only do women seldom need the release sexual and scatological joking brings, but few men appreciate hearing such humor from women. Any woman who thinks a tough mouth will help make her one of the boys, despite what Asimov says, is mistaken. One man describes a female attorney he deals with in his work as "one of the dirtiest-mouthed people I'm ever around." She's prone to dirty jokes and sexual gag gifts; she smokes and drinks and "really goes after it." Her colleague explains her behavior this way: "She's trying to be very aggressive; she used to be a teacher and is trying to break out of that mold. She's very insecure; that's why she's so bold and brash." He adds: "That behavior doesn't impress me at all." Loud and aggressive joking, especially sexual, is unwelcome, offensive behavior from any colleague, male or female. Women would do well to avoid trying to out-tough the guys.

LOVE AND WORK

Deflecting the jokes, handling colleagues who make uninvited advances, and trying to prevent men from seeing only sex when they look at you is important, of course. An equally troublesome situation, however, is: What if you are attracted to a man at work? Even the most inexperienced woman knows that getting sexually and emotionally involved with male colleagues is dangerous. And every novice has been advised to keep her love life and work life separate. That's sound advice, but not always easy to follow, particularly for single women.

Some women—usually those who are married and inclined toward monogamy—are very successful at keeping their love interests out of the office. Says one woman executive: "I always, always had an absolute rule that I never mixed my personal life or sex with anything at work. I knew instinctively to have an incest rule in the corporation."

There's no question that love affairs disrupt the workplace and that women still usually come out on the short end when such affairs go wrong—and sometimes even when they go right. In the *Harvard Business Review*, senior editor Eliza G. C. Collins wrote an article describing four case histories where "mature love" developed among executives. She explained how the relationship adversely affected the companies the men and women worked for. Her conclusion was that an organization's stability is threatened by such love and that top managers must take steps to deal with the consequences.

Among her recommendations is that the top manager must persuade one or both executives involved to leave. And if only one is to leave, it should be the one least essential to the organization. Collins calls the conclusion that somebody must go "painful" but "inevitable." And she recognizes that women are likely to be the least essential and thus more likely to lose their jobs. "Until more women are at high executive levels, the woman will usually be the prime victim when two executives fall in love, even if she is a senior member in the organization."

Obviously, women who are looking for romance would be better off finding it outside their workplaces. But that doesn't always happen. Daniela Kuper, head of Kuper Advertising, and a single mother, takes a more practical viewpoint: "For career women most of our lives are work, the rest of it we're cleaning our houses, doing our laundry, and looking after our children." If you don't hang out in singles places, you just may find romance in your business environment because that may be the only place you see men. "You have to be careful," she says, "but you also can't deny yourself a great life."

Being careful entails following three simple rules. First, no one-night stands with anyone related to work. Sleeping around gains a woman a reputation that swiftly undermines her professionalism. It also exposes her to many risks. For example, if the man didn't see the relationship as a one-time affair and feels rejected, he has powerful ammunition to get even and no sense of loyalty to hold him back. Those types of affairs have so little value that no woman serious about her career should find them worth the risks.

Second, avoid extramarital relationships, whether it's your marriage or his. The hottest, most intriguing office gossip usually involves who's sleeping with whom, especially if one of the parties is married. Romance between two single people is far less intriguing to the gossipmongers. Morality aside, cheating on a spouse is not something that gains anyone—male or female—respect in the business world.

Third, if you are single and do get involved with a close business associate, be discreet and private. Your romance is sure to threaten others and the less attention you draw to yourselves and the relationship the better. And don't be naive about what effects the relationship can have on your career. Few romances go on indefinitely or proceed to a smooth finish (marriage or dissolution) without one or both people changing jobs. Make sure he's worth the potential sacrifice.

10 TALKING MONEY

When Cheryl started work in 1975 as an assistant account executive, she was paid $2,000 less than a man from her class in college who was hired by the same advertising agency. Cheryl knew he was paid more, but it didn't worry her because she was quickly promoted and given a raise and he was not. "I was progressing faster and I thought 'This is great, it all depends on smarts,' " she says. "I didn't realize, however, how *much* better I was than that guy. And at the time I didn't connect with the idea that even though I was better than he was and was promoted over him, he was making the same money."

Many women have had similar experiences, though Cheryl's story has a happier ending than most. Now in her early thirties, she's making well over $100,000 a year—and has long since left her classmate behind. She overcame that $2,000 handicap in salary, but many women don't. Across the board, women continue to earn less—far less—than men: They average one-third less than men, earning $620 for every $1,000 that a man earns.

In any field you can point to—medicine, law, education, finance—men earn more than women. Even in jobs that are traditionally female, such as clerical positions, men earn more. That men get more money for the work they do is an indisputable fact that has been measured, analyzed, and argued from every angle. One study showed that female and male MBA graduates of Columbia University started out with the same salaries in 1970, but within ten years the women were earning just 81 percent of what the men were. Why do the salary differences exist? Explanations commonly offered include: women tend to work in low-paying fields; women don't have the same high level of skills and education that men do; and women lack the experience men have because women move in and out of the work force. But even when studies are done on groups of men and women who are the same in background, education, and experience, men come out ahead. And if education were the key to better pay, women would soon outpace men because women are rapidly becoming better educated than men. Women account for more than half of today's college students, and females are more likely to graduate from high school than are males. Nonetheless, no one is expecting to see women get a big pay boost.

Something else must account for the discrepancies. Although researchers can isolate specific variables—such as years in the work force or years of education—and measure those factors against salary, it is much more difficult to measure and identify the subtle influences, such as the reluctance of men in power positions to promote women into high-ranking jobs. Sex discrimination in pay is difficult to quantify, but plenty of research suggests it may be one of the most important reasons the pay gap exists. Anecdotal evidence to support the idea is easy to come by. Nudge almost any working woman and you'll hear a story of pay discrimination.

Anne, for example, worked at a company where men and women were given different titles for the same task: the women were called analysts, the men specialists and they were paid more. In another job Anne was the only nonclerical female in the company. Every time she got a promotion, which was about once a year, the company created a new title and position for her, giving her a separate, parallel track to the one the men were on. Management couldn't put Anne into the same jobs the men had because the pay was too high. Promoting her into a "man's" job would have meant almost doubling her salary. The men who concocted this plan for Anne were not malicious and didn't consciously set out to make sure she was paid less. In fact, the men felt pretty good about themselves; after all, they didn't expect Anne to be a secretary, like all the other women, and they were generous with promotions. They had a blind spot, however, one that many men have.

The blind spot is caused by a double standard that says women don't need or deserve as much money as men. It comes, in part, from the assumption that a woman's salary is the second one in the family and thus not as important as a man's. And maybe it comes also from the idea that money itself is too important, too significant in terms of power, to give to women. Judy, a lawyer, worked in a small firm with two male partners who were deaf to her requests for more money. They insisted that her salary was *very* good, even though it was less than Judy thought she should get for the job or could get elsewhere. Then one day, during a salary discussion, one of the partners pointed out to Judy what his wife, a secretary, earned, which was slightly less than what Judy was paid. Judy saw the whole problem in a new light after that. She realized that to the men it didn't matter that Judy was a lawyer. She was a *woman* and thus there was an unspoken cap on what she could earn.

Another woman was told a few years ago by a male mentor that she could expect to be making $20,000 in five years. He told her that in a kindly, encouraging way and expected her to be happy at the news. He made a six-figure salary, but even he, who respected this woman, who had promoted and defended and pushed her along as one of the new stars in the company, could not see that she was worth as much money as men were.

DANGERS IN BEING LOW-PAID

The immediate, obvious problem with earning less money than men is that you have less money—and less of everything that goes with money. Aside from the goods money can buy, you also lack the power that comes with money. The relationship between money and power is important throughout the work world, but it is especially obvious in politics. The cycle of powerlessness and the lack of money goes from female candidate to female supporter and back again. When Congresswoman Pat Schroeder first ran for Congress in 1972, there were two men of similar age and background also running for office. The national Democratic party took the men around to the political action committees and helped them each raise thousands of dollars. Schroeder got token amounts, because, as she said in an interview in *U.S. News and World Report*, the men "assumed a woman was a loser."

Asked why more women aren't in Congress, she said: "The answer is the color *green*—money." She contends that it is still hard for women to get the huge amounts of money necessary to run for major office. When she first ran, her average contribution was $7.50. "And many women still don't understand how much a political campaign costs," she said. "A woman might write me a check for $25, and her husband would write a $500 check to a male candidate."

The women Congresswoman Schroeder was talking about may simply be ignorant of how much a political campaign costs, but as long as they earn two-thirds (or less) of the salaries of their husbands, they'll also have less money to contribute even if they do wise up to the cost of political office. Not earning as much money as men hurts women—individually and collectively—in countless ways. It can even affect how women behave.

Psychologist and business consultant Baila Zeitz studied the problem-solving techniques of men and women in upper and middle management in thirty companies and made an interesting discovery about the relationship between behavior and pay. The study involved men and women who were all considered highly promotable by their companies and were similar in age, education, experience, and job levels. Nonetheless, the men were paid significantly more than the women. The few women who were paid higher salaries, salaries that compared favorably with the men's, behaved in the same confident, active way the men did. Women who were lower-paid, however, underestimated their problem-solving abilities and were less likely to assert themselves in group sessions or to disagree with others.

Another problem with being paid less is that women who are accustomed to having little money can be inclined to be cost-conscious when they shouldn't be. One woman, for instance, was told by a new boss not to worry about money—until further notice she was to spend whatever she needed to get the job done well. She refused to go outside her budget, however, saying she was sure that upper management would not approve of her boss's dictum.

Women can behave in stingy ways with their expense accounts as well. One of the few females in management in one company says she knows the men use their expense accounts differently from the way she does. "I'm very conservative and extremely honest. It's not that the men are dishonest, but they have a different idea about how to use expenses. They think that when you work for a big corporation the corporation should take care of you and you should be extremely comfortable when traveling on business—more comfortable than you would be if traveling for personal reasons. And I just can't do that." Her expense reports were singled out by her boss's boss, who told her male peers that he never had to question her reports, but frequently had to question theirs. One man, for example, rented a Cadillac on a busines trip; the woman always rents compacts. Getting singled out as the goody-goody did nothing for this woman's relationship with her peers—and didn't gain any respect from her bosses either. Men may say they don't want employees to spend excessively and they may mean it—but they also respect big spenders. They respect *money* and the people who have it and know how to use it.

WHAT MONEY MEANS TO MEN

Money has different meanings and more meaning to men than it does to women. Men measure success by money; they even measure themselves and their masculinity by money. Money helps define men. In contrast, having money or being overly concerned with money has until recently been considered unfeminine. Traditionally, it was not desirable for a woman to have money (especially *earned* money) because it made her too independent; a woman was expected to sit back and wait for a man to take care of her financially. Men, on the other hand, are often measured—by themselves and others—according to their earning powers. Psychiatrist Robert Gould writes of a male patient who had the idea that women were passive and wanted to be taken care of by a big, strong man. That idea required that the patient " 'make' good money before he could 'make' the woman of his dreams.'' Gould contends that men who are uncertain of their ability to attract women and who have a lot of self-doubt see money as a panacea. "For them,'' he writes, "money alone separates the men from the boys.''

Men who have an extreme reliance on money as a definer of self feel worthless when they don't have money and can react in strong ways to financial failures. Gould cites the case of a male stockbroker who lost a great deal of money in the market and become impotent. Even a temporary financial loss can render such a man helpless. "The most extreme and dramatic reaction to personal financial loss is suicide,'' writes Gould. "I have seen several men to whom great losses of money represented such a great loss of self, of ego, and ultimately of masculine image that life no longer seemed worth living.''

It is much harder to imagine a woman committing suicide over a financial failure. Money has less significance to a woman's ego.

Work and Money

Research shows consistent differences in the way the sexes—at almost any age—divide up the reward for a task between themselves and others. Females consistently pay themselves less than men do for whatever work or task the researcher sets up.

Various studies, some done on children as young as kindergarten age, others on adults and college students, are generally designed so that the subjects are asked to perform some task—such as answer questions or do math problems—while a fictitious partner in another room performs the same task. After the subject is finished, the researcher tells the subject whether he or she did better than, as well as, or less well than the partner. Then the subject is asked to divide some reward—money in the case of adults or some treat, like candies, in the case of children.

Females are consistently less opportunistic in the way they divide the reward. Generally, when the female is told she did a superior job on the task, she divides the reward equally; when males are told they did better, they divide the reward equitably, that is, in proportion to how much better they did on the task. When the partner's performance is superior, males once again divide the reward equitably. Women do the same, but generally take less for themselves than the men do. When the performance of subject and partner are equal, women once again take less for themselves than the males.

These findings usually don't surprise researchers; many begin the experiments expecting males, who are more aggressive, to maximize their gains at another's expense. Researchers have been surprised, however, at how little females take for themselves, even when they perform in a superior way to their partners.

There is much speculation about why the sexes differ in this way. One explanation is that females are more accommodating toward others, and, consistent with what we know about the psychology of females, they prefer to do whatever promotes harmonious relationships. Members of all-female groups, for instance, tend to divide a prize equally, regardless of differences in members' power. Males, on the other hand, are likely to divide a prize according to the power of each member of the group. Add a woman's preference for avoiding conflict to the weaker significance she places on money, and we can more easily understand why she might not care to take the biggest share of the reward for herself.

In 1979 two researchers, Charlene M. Callahan-Levy and Lawrence A. Messe, conducted a study to determine why women so consistently allocate less to themselves than males do. Their findings suggest another explanation: Females perceive less connection between their work and monetary rewards.

The researchers were testing the theories Phyllis Chesler and E. J. Goodman put forth in their 1976 book, *Women, Money and Power*: that is, compared to men, women see money as a less salient reward for the work they perform. Chesler and Goodman suggest that because females are not rewarded with money for their sex-role tasks (like mothering and housekeeping), they don't associate work with money. The assumption is that that attitude extends into other areas as well. Callahan-Levy and Messe suggest that because females may not make a connection between work and pay and pay and self-esteem, other factors influence their views of money. They may, for instance, be concerned with not seeming greedy and with appearing nice. Males, on the other hand, who see a more direct connection between their self-esteem and pay, are concerned primarily with getting what they think they deserve.

The more casual attitude many women have toward money, compared to the fervor with which many men approach it, is typified in the remarks of a married, childless marketing manager in her mid-thirties: "A lot of men spend what I think is entirely too much of their time making money. That's their goal in life and their wives take care of everything else. Not only do I not have a wife, but I don't want to live that way. Money is not that important to me. I've yet to meet a woman—although I'm sure there are some—who wants to make money as much as the men I know do."

A Weaker Sense of Worth

Although research demonstrating that males pay themselves more for work is plentiful, no one knows precisely why it is so. Psychologist Brenda Major, who has done much research on sex differences, writes that reward allocation is complex and likely to be influenced by a number of factors. Some of her research suggests that women expect lower salaries than men even when their qualifications are the same, and women think it fair to work longer and harder than men for the same amount of money. That suggests women simply expect less money for their work. The research of Callahan-Levy and Messe also provides strong evidence for the notion that women have lower expectations for their efforts or "a weaker sense of their own equity." They say that women "tend not to act in ways that maximally benefit them economically." In their experiments with pay allocation, Callahan-Levy and Messe found that although females paid themselves less, they also gave themselves high marks on performance. Thus, even though the women thought they had done a good job they still didn't pay themselves as well.

In their experiments Callahan-Levy and Messe also found that males not only allocated more pay to themselves, but saw a higher payment as being fair pay for the job. Both research and real-life evidence points strongly to the notion that women are willing to work for less money; men *expect* more and so they end up getting more. The wage-gap problem has two sides: Those in power (usually men) give women less money, but women also *accept* less, for a variety of reasons.

One woman says that the men in her company—who she is quite sure earn more than the women—exhibit high levels of confidence and expectation with regard to money. "I don't think that men fight any harder for money," she says. "For one thing it's easier for a boss to convince a woman that the company has been really good to her, but they just can't give her a raise now. But the men just exude an attitude that says, 'Hey, if I weren't here this company would be in trouble.' "

Women are filling many of the new low-paying service and office jobs, perhaps because they more than men are willing to work for low pay. Political scientist Andrew Hacker says that most men expect work that pays them a head-of-household wage, which is partly why women are finding it easier to get jobs these days than men—women take the less than head-of-household return that men refuse. Hacker suggests, for example, that since one airline reduced beginning pilot salaries to $18,000, which is less than what senior flight attendants get, we can expect to see fewer male pilots on that airline. Women will take the jobs at salaries men won't.

WOMEN, AGGRESSION, AND MONEY

The reasons women work for less money are necessarily complex. Many causes are external to women themselves. Women not only expect less, but they command less in the job market. Because women are discriminated against and often denied power, money, and advancement, they sometimes *must* take lower-paying jobs. Being a pilot at $18,000 a year is better than not being a pilot at all, which may be the only other option for a woman trying to break into a male field. Working at a low-paying service job that a man wouldn't take is better than not having a job at all, particularly if you have a couple of children to support. Getting a promotion without a raise is preferable to getting neither.

The fight to change the social structures that encourage lower pay for women won't be won overnight. In the meantime, individual women can help themselves by monitoring their own behavior. Too often women make it easy for others to deny them money. Consultant Denise Cavanaugh says she sees women who are sometimes so grateful and eager to get a job that they don't worry about the pay—until they get into the position and learn that men are making more money. Cavanaugh says that when it comes to asking for money, men are like the lizards that puff themselves up to twice their size to frighten off enemies. Men can make themselves seem bigger and better than they are—and the act is convincing. Women tend not to do that and often regret their lack of bravado. One woman, a lawyer, says that when she worked in her state attorney general's office she was working for less money than she had to. "I think I would have been able to get more money if I had been aware of salaries and if I had tried for more," she says. "Instead I sat back and waited for the regular raises. I didn't pay the attention that I should have—especially at the entry level."

A woman who heads her own business observes that the men who work for her seem to have a better sense of what they're worth than the women do and the men ask for more. She says she thinks the women secretly fear they'll jeopardize their jobs by making demands—and it is painful to her to see women behave that way. The lack of aggression that women demonstrate with regard to money is equally evident to men. One man who teaches at a university says that the women he works with grumble about pay a lot but don't do

anything about getting more, such as going after grants and negotiating salaries. "I think women are less aggressive about getting
money," he says. "They more easily accept lower pay than men
do."

Part of the reason women accept less is that they are less wise in
the ways of business. Specifically, they often think they're not supposed to have to ask for money. One woman proudly announced
that in more than twenty years of working she had never had to ask
for raises, but had always gotten them. On another occasion she
complained that a male friend who was almost ten years younger
and had a position similar to hers at a smaller company was making
more money. She was oblivious to the connection between her passivity and the amount of her salary. Had she puffed herself up like
a lizard at raise time, she might be earning more.

Spotting Discrimination

The first step a woman must take toward getting parity with men is
to recognize when she's discriminated against—and surprisingly enough
that's not as easy as it sounds. Faye Crosby, a professor of psychology at Yale University, conducted a study of working men and
women to discover what factors contribute to a sense of gratification
or grievance. She found it particularly intriguing that women seemed
unable to see discrimination against themselves, even though they
thought *other* women were discriminated against. Paradoxically,
women said they felt satisfied by conditions that were obviously
unsatisfactory.

The study involved a group of 163 women and 182 men who were
matched in background, job status, motivation, and job satisfaction.
In the groups of men and women there were equal proportions of
people in high-status jobs, like doctors, lawyers, and business consultants, and low-status jobs, such as clerks. The men, however,
earned an average of $8,000 to $10,000 more than the women. And
yet the women, like the men, reported they were satisfied and fairly
treated in all aspects of their jobs, *including pay*. The women said

they thought sex discrimination in the American labor force was strong and that men and women received unequal pay for equal work; they simply didn't think they specifically were suffering from discrimination. Crosby says that the women in her study seemed to follow an "unspoken syllogism. It starts with the major premise: 'Women are discriminated against.' It continues with the minor premise: 'I am a woman.' And in a burst of psychologic it concludes: 'Phew, that was a close call.' "

The inability of women to see discrimination when it applies to themselves is not something peculiar to the female sex; it's part of human nature. We all like to feel exempt from the unpleasant aspects of life, and we block out realities that prevent us from feeling exempt. Telling about a man who started work at her company at a lower level and at higher pay, a woman said, "It just happened that way. I don't speculate about it because to do so would make me unhappy."

Some women who appear to be blind to discrimination against themselves may not necessarily be avoiding the unpleasant truth; perhaps they simply don't know what others are paid. It's one thing to be aware of the broad issue of sex discrimination and quite another to know what the fellow in the next office is getting paid.

Asking for More, Getting More

The most important change a woman can make in her behavior is to recognize when she's paid too little and to ask for more. She'll gain both respect and money. Statistics suggest that women who do want or need more, get more. Political scientist Andrew Hacker points out that divorced women tend to have higher salaries than married women. He says that may be because divorced women are more likely to make pay a primary consideration in their choice of jobs. Talking about her career change, one divorced woman said, "I started my own business because I was on my own and had two kids and I realized what a schnook I was for not making much money."

Women entrepreneurs often learn quickly that they must—and

can—push themselves to ask for and expect good pay. One started a consulting business and discovered that she had to raise her fees as she gained more prestigious clients in order to maintain a respected position among her competitors. She knew that clients who were used to paying high prices for consultants would see her not as a bargain, but as unworthy if she priced herself too low. She taught herself to use what she calls her "toe-curling rule." When she's face-to-face with a client, if the fee she names makes her toes curl, then it's probably high enough. Even using her toe-curling rule, she has yet to set a price so high that a client balked.

The more experience, confidence, and success a woman gains, the easier it is for her to get paid what she's worth. Another entrepreneur says, "As I have increased my own self-esteem and gotten my feet on the ground, I've been able to establish some firm limits for myself. I can say to a client, 'This is going to cost you $2,000. If you don't like the fee I'm prepared to lose you. You can walk.' The first two years in business I didn't dare do that. I was never good at poker and I couldn't refuse to negotiate a fee when I had no money in the bank. To do that seems very male to me, and it's something I just couldn't do at first. It took me time and some success before I could be tough in money negotiations."

Women do themselves a service when they learn to employ some of the bravado that seems to come so easily to men. A business consultant encourages women when job-hunting to assume that their current salaries are low and to compensate for that by asking more than they normally would. She also encourages them to think expansively about their work experience; it's okay, for example, to say you're experienced at something even if you've only done it once. The stronger a woman feels, the more easily she can ask for the pay she is worth.

11 GETTING AND USING POWER

Most conflicts between men and women in the workplace come down to power struggles: Women want more power; men hold and closely guard most of it. Many differences between the sexes are also power differences. Male language is the language of the powerful; the way men use sex in the office is a way of exerting dominance over women; even male humor is more aggressive and more inclined to give men power. Learning to spot power plays, to develop a powerful work style, and to seize power requires that a woman draw on all her knowledge of men and how they operate.

POWER—A MALE PREROGATIVE?

Men are so accustomed to vying with other men for power that they tend not to consider women as part of the battle. In some instances, that's because women traditionally have held subordinate roles and men have grown accustomed to seeing women as inferior. In a large hospital in Colorado, for example, all the high-level administrators were male except one, and she was in charge of the nurses. And even though she represented a much larger group of people than the other administrators, her position was relatively powerless. She was in charge of *nurses*—in other words, women—and in a hospital dominated by men that was an unimportant role.

The nurse administrator's powerlessness flowed down and resulted in powerlessness for the supervisors, mostly women, who worked for her. Says one: "Most of my management problems and frustrations had to do with budgets and staffing, because the nursing administrator had no clout and couldn't deliver what we needed. Her leverage within the overall hospital administration was not good. A large group of women—nurses—were competing for a limited amount of resources against a fairly small group of men. And invariably the women came out on the bottom.'' When the nurse administrator tried to increase her influence and make the hospital system more responsive to the requirements of her staff, she was forced out of her job.

One reason men insist on having power is that they have come to think of it as their just due. After all, society hands it to them right and left—children take their father's names, women are "given" in marriage by their parents to their husbands, grandfathers sit at the heads of holiday dinner tables. The ways in which men are routinely and thoughtlessly awarded power and authority are innumerable; for instance, men are chosen to be jury foremen much more frequently than women, and far out of proportion to the number of men who serve on juries.

Men acquire a lot of power through default; just because they're male we expect them to hold the reins. Women, on the other hand, have to earn—and often fight for—whatever power they get. All other factors being equal, a woman, simply by being female, is less powerful than a man.

Males and male characteristics are in many ways more valued in our culture and thus males have higher status, one of the marks of power. Men generally control more resources, have more expertise and confidence, all-important factors in determining how much power a person has. The characteristics of power match the stereotypes of masculinity: We use words such as "strong," "potent," "dominant," and "aggressive" to describe powerful people. Masculine images are used to denote power: One man might describe another he admires as "a man with his hand on the throttle." The feminine voice and image are seldom used to convey strength and power. Most radio and television advertisements, for example, even those directed at women, use male voices because that is the accepted and expected voice of authority. When women do get power they are sometimes identified with men. A magistrate in a midwestern city says she's grown accustomed to being called "Sir" by defendants who come before her in her courtroom. People—men and women —are so used to seeing males in positions of authority that many can't adjust when faced with a woman.

Men also expect power because they need it; it's essential to their manliness. To feel good about themselves, men need to be able to exercise power. Michael Korda (*Power! How to Get It, How to Use It*) says the need is "constant and almost instinctive." Men learn it in school, playing sports, and in the military. He adds: "It's part of their make-up, a sense of power is natural to them if they have any intelligence and ambition. . . . And since they think of power as a male prerogative, their fiercest games are fought with women."

Although men may be willing to yield certain powers and authority to women—on the home front, for example—they will strongly resist doing so at work, which men consider their domain. Power in the workplace is both more necessary to men and better understood by them. Korda says that men almost intuitively understand that power games and politicking are as important as doing the work, whereas women generally don't. That makes it all the easier for men to keep power from women.

Barriers to Power

One of the tactics men have for denying women power is to diminish any position held by a woman. Any job a woman does, Korda explains, is downgraded as soon as it's evident she can do it. He makes the extreme suggestion that if a woman were elected President of the United States and a male elected Vice President, we'd see the Vice Presidency turned into a powerful position and the Presidency diminished until the two were treated as a team of equals. While it is unlikely that a head of state would suffer such a fate, many female managers have been given the titles but not the authority that went with the job under a male predecessor.

Another way men keep women from gaining power is by condescending to them when they do attain responsible positions. Men often refuse to grant women the opportunity to prove their abilities. Men who engage in such protectionism frequently rationalize that they are doing a woman a favor by guarding her from potential pitfalls. American Express's Meredith Fernstrom says, "There is a patronizing attitude among some men who feel they shouldn't give a woman a big challenge in a new assignment because if she fails then they have contributed to her failure somehow. They'll give the big risks to the boys who they figure can make it or break it."

Often a man's intentions are directly self-interested. He may resist giving a woman more responsibility for fear of being associated with her should she fail. One woman who has come up through the ranks in the computer industry was both helped and hurt by a male mentor who did just that. "It was the favorite-child syndrome," she says. "He was afraid his child would fail. It put a great strain on me because sometimes I *do* fail. But I felt I wasn't allowed to." She thinks he was protecting himself—not as an unkindness and not even consciously. If a man sticks his neck out for a woman, who then turns out not to be up to standard, he has risked more than if a man he promoted or sponsored had failed. That's because some of his male colleagues may have considered his placing a woman in a responsible position to reflect a lack of judgment—and her failure just proves them right.

Men also deny women responsibility because they want to protect their own power bases. For example, if a woman is gaining strength, men might withdraw their support for her by permitting others in the office to criticize her, by diffusing her area of responsibility, by denying her access to critical meetings, or by promoting someone over her, thus sending a signal throughout the company that she is no longer held in high regard. A woman at a cable television company, for example, had attained a coveted position on the team of deal-makers for the company, but then had trouble doing her job because the men deliberately excluded her. On one occasion the men knew about a party where executives from a client company would be. The men attended but deliberately kept word of the event from the woman.

Some of the forces that keep women from attaining power come from within women themselves. Unlike men, according to psychologist Jean Baker Miller, women don't have a history of believing that power is essential to their self-image. Although the ability to build a power base is essential to success, for example, most don't have a psychological makeup that leads them to want subordinates. In addition, they are likely to lack experience in using and fighting for power. The rivalries and countless rounds of competition that males engage in from childhood on prepare them well for the power struggles at work.

Women don't like—or learn how—to vie for power. Instead of unhesitantly going for leadership positions and exerting status and power over others, they are more inclined to neutralize status distinctions. They are more egalitarian in their approach to others, and they often don't press the advantage when in positions of power.

Psychoanalyst Ethel Spector Person says that misunderstanding power is characteristic of even some successful women. For instance, if a woman disagrees with her boss at a meeting she may be surprised to find out he's furious at her insubordination. Her preference for equality can get in her way both by preventing her from grabbing opportunities to be a leader and thus superior to others, and by preventing her from understanding her proper role in a power hierarchy. Says one high-ranking female executive, "Women often don't understand how important it is to the CEO and to everyone around him that you be deferential. Women don't realize that when the CEO flickers his eyelash you're expected to jump to attention."

Even more common, Person says, is a literal misunderstanding of the dynamics of power. "The overriding focus on affiliative ties," she writes, "obscures the reality of power relations." A woman is apt to confuse her relationship with a powerful person with power held in her own right. Women who hope to advance in their careers can't let themselves be content with getting close to powerful people; they must want and acquire power of their own.

Getting power isn't easy for women because they start from a position of assumed powerlessness. Psychologists Florence Geis and Natalie Porter tested a well-established leadership cue, one that says the person sitting at the head of a table is the authority figure in a group, to discover whether the cue held for women as well as men. The research turned up some bad news. In the study, more than 400 subjects observed a series of seating arrangements and judged the leadership of group members. In all instances the head-of-table effect held, that is, the person seated at the head was seen as the group leader, *except* when a woman was at the head of the table in a mixed-sex group. Sex-role stereotypes overrode the leadership cues, and women were seen as leaders only when there wasn't a man available for the role.

Unfortunately, gaining power isn't as simple as just watching the men and adopting their behavior. Working women must overcome a great many prejudices to be seen as powerful. The forces that keep power from women are insidious, whether they come from men who are intentionally trying to diminish a woman, from cultural stereotypes, or from a woman's own psyche, but the situation isn't hopeless. You *can* get power—it just won't be easy.

Types of Power

Power comes in many forms and can even be disguised as weakness. If you had a flat tire, for instance, and wanted someone else to change it, you could appear helpless and have little trouble getting the first man who happened along to get his hands dirty. Women have traditionally used that sort of manipulation to get men to do what they want. Women have been expected to be indirect in their uses of power, because the traditional dominance order puts men on top and women in subordinate positions. Thus, women have had to learn to be powerful from a secondary position. Many men find women who are blatantly powerful to be offensive. The authors and

editors of *Women and Sex Roles: A Social Psychological Perspective*
offer the following exchange as an example of the differing expectation for power use by men and women:

A male medical resident on duty at a hospital is called at 1 A.M.
by a nurse who tells him a patient (not one of his) is unable to sleep
because she learned of her father's death that day.

The doctor replies: "What sleeping medication has been helpful
to Mrs. Brown in the past?" (By phrasing the question that way the
doctor can ask the nurse for a recommendation without appearing,
to either of them, to be doing so.)

The nurse replies: "Pentobarbital mg 100 was quite effective night
before last."

He responds: "Pentobarbital mg 100 as needed for sleep; got it?"
The nurse dutifully thanks him.

She could have just called the resident and said that Mrs. Brown
needs a sleeping pill, would he okay a dose of Pentobarbital? In
keeping with her subordinate position, however, she took a less direct
approach. Although in this case, the nurse's behavior may have been
appropriate since doctors are of higher status and nurses aren't supposed to prescribe medicine, the editors of *Women and Sex Roles*
point out that the doctor/nurse game is played out by women and
men in all sorts of situations, to the detriment of women. Women
who are trying to gain status and power should avoid such tactics at
work. They only reinforce in men's minds the subordinate position
of women and deny women the sense of power; if a woman doesn't
feel powerful, she can't even begin to *be* powerful.

Another type of indirect power used by women is referent power,
in which influence is solicited through personal appeals such as
"because we're friends" or "because we're in this together." The
success of such an appeal depends upon the person being influenced
finding the influencer likable and *similar*. Although this type of
power is often used by women, it is not very effective in the workplace. That's because men sometimes don't *want* to identify with
women (and their generally lower status) or because they just *can't*

identify with women (whom they see as entirely different from themselves).

Women can, and often do, effectively use expert power, which is based on having the experience or knowledge that is needed by others. Making sure you know what others need to know is a difficult, but lasting way, of gaining power.

Men are more likely than women to use reward and coercion to assert power. That tactic is generally used by someone who already holds real power, because its success depends on the ability of the person posing a threat to actually carry it out. Men are more likely to use this technique because they are more likely to be the keepers of the "yes/no" power. But women can use it too, even women who don't possess real power.

Perceived power, the power others think you have whether you do or not, can be as effective as real power. In fact, much more business is done on the basis of perceived power than real power. If you're the head of your own company, for example, you have a great deal of real power within your firm—you're the ultimate holder of the yes/no, hire/fire, buy/sell power—and you have little need for perceived power. With those outside your own company, though, you may need both real and perceived power. Employees also can possess and need both types of power; for instance, they may have real power over subordinates, but also a great deal of perceived power with them, as well as with peers and superiors. Men often operate on perceived power. They seem to know that you don't actually have to have power to act as if you do. But then they also are more likely to be seen as powerful when they're not, just because they're men.

Women have more trouble with perceived power, but they can learn to use and acquire it. But to do that requires risk-taking and strong action. If the other person sees through your bluff, you're done for. Charlene tells about a situation where she effectively used perceived power with a colleague whose work was not satisfactory. Charlene covered for him on a last-minute project that required late hours to finish correctly and on time. When the crisis passed, Charlene called the man into her office and said, "I care about what my name goes on and I care about the quality of the work that leaves this office. If you don't, then get out." His reply: "I'm not going to take your talking to me like that, I'm going to our boss."

Charlene seized the moment and exercised power she wasn't sure she possessed. She said, "Fine, but you'd better play that game to win, because based on the quality of your work you'll never be picked over me."

The strategy worked because the man did not go to the boss and his work improved. To gain control over the situation, Charlene herself went to the boss and told him about the situation; she told him she needed his backing and he gave it to her. By wielding power she wasn't certain she had, she ended up getting it.

Seizing Power

Women can't wait to be granted power or to be invited into the ranks of the powerful: They have to fight for opportunities. But they don't always do it. When the vice president in charge of a large division was fired, several women on the staff were in positions high enough that they rightfully should have expected to be considered for the job; only one approached top management (all male) to express her ambitions. The only male in a high staff position, however, went straightaway to the top brass to find out whether he would be in the running. When he learned that the company expected to hire from the outside, he promptly found a job—and a promotion—with a competitor. The women, who were passed over, are all still on staff in the same positions.

Women gain power not only by getting promotions but by widening their areas of responsibility within current jobs. And those are the very actions that bring women into conflict with the men who resist women's gaining authority. Marilyn works in a young, aggressive company on the West Coast in the entertainment business. One department in the firm is, as Marilyn says, "a boy's club." That's where the deals are made. "I, like every other MBA who entered that company, took one look and said, 'Oh, I want to be in *that* department,' " she says. Over time she developed a good relationship with the members of the group and was working her way in. "I could feel their respect when I walked into the room to work with them. But there was an imaginary line which I could not cross. It was okay for me to be in the position of *helping*, of getting information and advising them on negotiations, but it wasn't okay to do more."

Then one day Marilyn saw her opportunity to gain ground; her hope was to become a regular participant in negotiations involving deals between her company and others. A deal-making meeting was coming up with some people from a movie studio and it happened that Marilyn knew one of the principals—the very person her company wanted to make the deal with. "It was great," says Marilyn. "We kissed each other on the cheeks when he came in, and when the whole group went to lunch I sat next to him. I was thinking to myself, 'If there was any doubt in their minds that they would be comfortable with me during this negotiation or that I would be comfortable sitting here with all these people, it should be erased today.' "

She was feeling great when she walked into the meeting room early the next morning, before the studio people arrived, to take her place at the negotiating table. Then, she says, "the man I had worked for all these years and who I thought really respected me, looked at me and said, 'There's no need for you to be here today; your lawyer counterpart will take over.' " To Marilyn, the remark was clearly an excuse to get her out. "*I was crushed*," she says. "This was something I had worked up to for a long time." She left the room without argument. Later she learned that male peers—in exactly the same job she held—routinely participated in negotiations.

Marilyn let herself be victimized by a power play that was all too easy for her male superior to carry off. Had she been more experienced with men and power, she might have anticipated her boss's move and countered it even before he tried to cut her out. And she certainly would have seen his comment as the simple power play it was when it did come. Feeling "crushed" prevented her from fighting back and made her want to flee instead. She might have won some ground had she been able to say pleasantly and seemingly innocently, "Oh, I'd like to stay; I'm gathering material that will be helpful in preparing my financial report next week." He probably didn't want to get into an open struggle with her and may not have insisted she leave because he had no good reason to exclude her. But he got rid of her easily with one comment. By gently resisting his rejection, she might have been able to stay in the meeting and set a precedent for future negotiations.

Women have to realize that they start from a position of the subordinated. Thus, as a first step to gaining power, women must resist male attempts at control and limitation. That's not easy because, writes psychologist Jean Baker Miller, dominant groups "tend to characterize even subordinates' initial small resistance to dominant control as demands for an excessive amount of power!"

Not easy, but it can be done, as Roberta, a mid-level manager in a large corporation, discovered. A major project she had been working on for months was heating up and gaining the attention of high-ranking men in her company. Because her boss had a tendency to step in and seize her projects at critical moments, Roberta decided that this time she wouldn't let it happen.

A big meeting that would determine the direction of the project was coming up and, based on past experience, Roberta had reason to fear her boss would decide he should be present—and in charge. To head that off, she went to him several days before the meeting and laid out her plan for the project. She spoke confidently of her strategies and displayed her knowledge of the many nuances of the problem. She ended the discussion with her boss by saying firmly, "I'll get back to you first thing Friday morning to report on the meeting."

Her tactics worked; her boss stayed away. By being alert to the circumstances in which her boss was likely to deny her power, Roberta successfully kept control of her work and gained power.

MALE LEADERSHIP IS NOT INEVITABLE

Although males are more aggressive than females, aggression is not necessarily helpful to either sex in gaining power and leadership roles. Aggression is useful among children to establish rank, but among adults influence of others takes place through more complex and diverse forces.

Research reported by Maccoby and Jacklin in *The Psychology of Sex Differences* indicates that in groups of children, those who are good athletes and are physically strong have an edge in dominating others, although popularity and attractiveness are also important. As children grow older, leadership qualities become more diverse; adolescents who try to dominate peers purely through toughness are seldom accepted. By college age there is some evidence that male leaders are more authoritarian in their own groups than females are in theirs, but maintaining leadership depends increasingly on being effective in achieving the group's goals.

On the job, complex interactions are even more important. Although leadership does call for a certain toughness, a devotion to purpose and an ability to keep others fixed on the group's goals matter as well; interpersonal aggression is seldom needed. In fact, it can be detrimental to a group's function. Maccoby and Jacklin suggest that as males and females grow into adulthood and as leadership comes to depend more on competence and mutual attraction, "equality of the sexes in power-bargaining encounters becomes possible."

Dominance relationships fluctuate depending on competence, motivation, and commitment of each person to the relationship. Dominance in adulthood can be achieved through such nonaggressive means as flattery, bribery, deception, persuasion, personality, bargaining, reasoning, and affection. Thus, Maccoby and Jacklin conclude, there's nothing inevitable about male achievement of "all available leadership positions." When such skills as setting goals, planning, organizing, and persuading are called for, there's no reason to select men over women for leadership positions.

Why aren't more women in positions of power then? Because there's something else going on between women and men that gives men an advantage in gaining power. Maccoby and Jacklin speculate that the reason certain jobs (such as leadership positions) have traditionally gone to men is not so much because those jobs require aggressiveness, as because women "being slower to anger, are less likely to protest onerous assignments . . . girls are more likely than boys to comply with demands that adults make upon them; although it has not been demonstrated, it appears likely that in adulthood as well they will 'take orders' from authority figures with less coercion. To put the matter bluntly, they are easier to exploit." Being easy to exploit is, quite obviously, something any woman seeking to achieve positions of authority would do well to avoid.

Being compliant and easy to get along with are not necessarily negative traits, but women who tend toward that behavior have to be careful to keep their eyes on their objectives. Grace, an accountant in a large firm, lost sight of her goals and let herself be exploited by her fellow accountants, all male. They weren't malicious, they merely found it easy to say, "Ask Grace; she'll do it." And Grace would. For example, last year the firm acquired personal computers for the accountants, and it was Grace who saw to it that the software was adapted to the needs of the firm; that took up a lot of her time over several weeks. Then she noticed that none of the tax forms had been ordered and the season was almost upon them so she did the ordering. She was rapidly becoming the office manager with the encouragement of her colleagues. Then one day her boss, one of the partners, called her in for a conference. "Grace," he said, "your billings are lower than anyone else's. What are you going to do about that?" Her billings were low, of course, because she was spending her time with chores she didn't own and at the same time freeing up the men to spend more and more time doing what they were paid to do—accounting. She let herself be swept up in the pleasures of being the one others could count on, and in the process lost sight of what her goal should have been.

If a woman focuses on what she needs to do to get ahead and do her job well, she'll find it easier to say no when someone tries to deflect her—no matter how gently or nicely they do it.

Managing Others' Perceptions

Successful women who *do* have power are the first to say they didn't get it by "letting it all hang out." Except for the few who dominate through sheer force of personality or exceptional resources (such as inherited wealth or position), most have to strive to create images for themselves and to guide others into seeing them as powerful. One entrepreneur says that over time she has "refined" her approach in asserting power with men. Another in the corporate world says she has learned that what is important to success is how people perceive your performance. You must, she says, learn to "manage those perceptions."

A magistrate in a midwestern city says she behaves in specific and deliberate ways in order to achieve and maintain the power she requires to do her job well. She says she finds it important to "maintain a sense of awe" so that the emotions and behavior of others don't get out of control in the courtroom. To do that she will, for example, occasionally shout or be very cold, taking on a stern expression. "I think of it as acting and it does have an effect on people," she says. With other accouterments of power—her black robe, gavel, and courtroom bench that places her higher than the lawyers and litigants who come before her—she retains the power that goes with her position.

Successful women have learned to develop a power style they are comfortable with. There's no specific formula that works for all women; each needs to find one that suits her personality. Many acquire power by being strong and patient, controlled and decisive, by wielding and seizing power in low-key ways. Martha Layne Collins, governor of Kentucky, for example, says her political style is to work quietly behind the scenes. "I've been able to accomplish a lot of things from a surprise approach," she said in an interview in *The New York Times.* "It's kind of like you don't know what's happening to you until it happens." Gannett's Madelyn Jennings has an easygoing, humane style. "A straight spine and a sense of humor are the last things to lose," she says. "I think we can bring much to the male bastions. We can bring to positions of power an increased sense of humanity. We can enhance the people with whom we work, and we'll emerge as *leaders* because we're genuinely capable of helping people perform at their optimum level. And that is what the art of managing is all about."

Occasionally, women do succeed by using force. One young entrepreneur, who built a multimillion-dollar commercial real estate business from nothing, has achieved much of her power through sheer persistence and determination. Her will enabled her to press on, no matter how many people said "no" when she was starting her business. She still engages in few subtleties in her dealings with men. When a sale was threatened because the client insisted on a $57,000 down payment and the buyer wanted to pay only $50,000, the entrepreneur told the buyer: "Don't be so difficult. There are bigger and better things to worry about." He paid the extra $7,000 and the sale went through. She can afford to be abrupt because she has control of what others want.

In order to be perceived as powerful, women must take deliberate and careful steps to acquire as many powerful characteristics as they can. Fighting macho with macho is usually futile, but women can cultivate powerful manners and an effective personal style of dealing with others. Women need all the ammunition they can gather—from firm speech and power-oriented body language to a confident attitude that discourages exploitation. Women must operate consciously to seize power and to project images of authority and control.

What the Powerful Possess

Even though different power styles can be effective for women, there are certain characteristics the powerful share, and others that the powerful never possess. The first step for women toward gaining power, according to Katharine Graham, chairman and CEO of The

Washington Post Company, is "to shed those traits that persist from the days when they were truly second-class citizens. One is being too perfectionist—too detail-oriented, compelled to dot every 'i' and cross every 't,' but oblivious of the big picture. Another is reluctance to delegate responsibility. A third is the desire to please."

The concern women have for affiliations with others sometimes leads them to wish to please and be liked. But, as one woman entrepreneur says, "The key to success is not getting people to like you. That's not what business is about. Clients have to respect you and believe in your ability. They don't have to like you." A woman whose goal is to be powerful can't set about becoming popular. She may end up being both powerful and well-liked, but she won't get there by trying to please others above all else.

Controlling and being in command of the details is not what brings a person power either. People at low levels, who are paid to attend to the details more powerful people shun, must be experts at managing the nitty-gritty or they'll lose their jobs. But many women at higher levels worry more about detail than is good for their careers. One such who works in the finance department of a large company says that the responsibility for pulling together the final report on a project usually goes to a woman. And the report is always better when a woman does it. The women, she says, are more thorough and complete in their work. They make sure the secretary orders thirty-five black ring binders; they coordinate the typists so that the material is ready on time; they pull all the pieces together efficiently and expertly. But they gain nothing by taking on that time-consuming task. It's not a prestigious task—and it is one that men avoid. The men know it's the deals, not the details, that get you somewhere.

The chairman and chief executive officer of a large bank, one of the world's most powerful bankers, exemplifies the executive who considers operational details—even vital ones—to be none of his concern. He says he's probably the only CEO of a bank in the United States who doesn't know at any given moment what the prime interest rate is.

Being able to let go of the details goes along with two other

characteristics of the powerful. One is that successful people understand that working on important projects signals that you're an important person. Many on-the-job power struggles involve turf battles;
anyone who is ambitious wants the most important and largest area
of responsibility. The rest is left to less savvy workers.

The other principle that successful people see as critical to using
power is being able to share power and delegate authority and tasks.
As one highly placed woman says, "You never really have power
until you can share it with others." Only those who are unsure of
their power and fearful of losing it will hoard what they have and
be miserly with peers and subordinates.

The powerful also know that having access to both formal and
informal sources of information is vital to maintaining and increasing
power. Says one man in government, "Power is simply knowing
what's going on. Knowing, for example, who likes whom, who
doesn't like whom, who needs to get something done, who can wait,
who has a need for certain kinds of attention or advice. If you know
people's needs, peculiarities, and biases, then you probably are going
to be able to have an impact on their activities without their feeling
that you're dominating or manipulating. If you can't find things out,
if people won't tell you things, you'll never get anywhere."

Women usually have to be more alert and opportunistic than a
man in order to uncover what they need to know. That's because
women have less access to the informal networks of information,
particularly those that come through social situations, as described
in Chapter 7. Because power is more difficult for women to come
by, they must be more conscious of power relationships, power
behavior, and power plays.

Useful Power Plays

Although we know from experience and experiment that women can't
appear powerful simply by adopting the behavior of powerful men,
women can shed verbal and nonverbal cues that project insecurity
and subordination. Women also can enhance their power by culti-

vating power traits. You may not automatically be awarded the power of a group leader by simply taking the head seat at the meeting table, but you may if you take the head seat *and* speak firmly *and* have the information critical to the task at hand *and* keep hands and eyes steady.

You should also have some small power plays in your repertoire, ready to pull out for a man who needs a reminder of your strength. Used judiciously and in concert with the principles outlined above, they can help a woman accumulate power.

- Use time as a power weapon. Keeping another person waiting reduces their stature and enchances yours. There is indignity in waiting. That's why, for example, the airlines have a separate line for first-class passenger check-in. Unlike hoi polloi, high-status and high-powered people are not expected to spend their time waiting—others are supposed to wait on them. Don't, however, keep someone waiting so long that your behavior is unmistakably rude—you'll then be forced to apologize and thereby hand the waitee an advantage.
- Stand whenever you can in dealings with others. You'll appear more forceful and energetic.
- Take people by surprise. Step into someone's office unannounced if you can get past the secretary. Be cheerful and friendly so the person caught off guard can't easily put you down with a quick dismissal. When you are expected, knock and walk quickly into the room, giving the person seated at his desk little time to respond.
- Acknowledge power plays from others. It will help diffuse the effect of the dominance assertion, and it will let others know you understand what's going on. For example, you can disarm a man who is sending body language signals indicating he is closed to what you're saying. If he's frowning and sitting with arms folded tight across his chest, try saying something like, "You look puzzled," or, "I see you're still unsure about this,"

or, "You seem not to want to hear this." Such comments will put him off guard, because even though he wanted to give you that message nonverbally, he didn't want his feelings out in the open—and he'd certainly rather not explain them.

Cultivate dominance and leadership behavior and encourage other women to do likewise. The more men get used to seeing women using power signals at work, the more likely the behavior will be effective for women generally.

THE POWER MYSTIQUE

As early as junior high school, girls are reminded by mothers and older sisters that little boys aren't as tough as they seem—they cry, too. In high school we are told that the boys are just as frightened of calling us for dates as we're afraid they won't call. And now that you're in the working world, you're hearing that men are vulnerable just as women are. We had trouble believing it in junior high, just as we do now—but it is so. Men display a lot of bravado that can disarm women, but men have their worries, insecurities, and fears, too. It helps to remember that when doing business with them. Keeping in mind that men can be insecure helps you feel strong and can prevent you from awarding them any extra power.

No matter how powerful or accomplished a man is, he has his weaknesses. Getting even a glimpse of them puts men in a different light. At a press conference in New York City, former cabinet member, U.S. Attorney General, and onetime Ambassador to England Elliot Richardson presided over a large group of journalists from major publications and broadcast studios. Richardson gave a short presentation; he then joined the other panelists, who were seated in swivel chairs on the stage, while the television cameras were readied for the press conference. Richardson crossed his legs and when he did so his pants hiked up, exposing a stretch of leg between his trousers and socks. He looked at his leg and, not knowing his microphone was open, said, "Oh, dear, I should have worn high socks; these look terrible." An uncomfortable titter went through the room. No one wanted that glimpse of Richardson, and because he still didn't realize his mike was on, no public joke could be made to diffuse the tension.

Because men are men and thus pull more power and prestige than women whether they earn it or not—and because they know so well how to seem gruff and in control whether they are or not—we tend to assume they're secure and comfortable in their power. One man, cool and distant as they come, does a great deal of business over lunch with clients. He admits to being uncomfortable when a client wants to get right down to business. He prefers to chitchat first, especially about baseball. That's not because he wants to control the conversation or find out something about the client before doing business or any other strategic power motive. He prefers it simply because he's afraid he won't have enough to talk about. He doesn't make small talk easily (except about baseball) and has a limited number of projects to discuss with any one client. He's fearful of being caught in the middle of the entrée with coffee and dessert yet to come and nothing left to say.

A highly placed woman in a large corporation, who knows how strong the power mystique can be, makes a point of getting to know young women in the company who show promise. She tries to spend some time with them and let them see her in action, deliberately trying to be a role model. Part of her purpose is to show those women that they can be comfortable with someone who is powerful. The executive is higher and more powerful than any of the men the young women work for. She hopes that if they see that what separates them from the men is often mere mystique and style, they'll relax around men too. Being relaxed is the first step on the way to being powerful and in control.

12 CLOSING THE CREDIBILITY GAP

A recent advertisement touts cotton boxer shorts and tank T-shirts for women with the headline: "Did you ever think you'd be so at ease in a man's world?" The copy reads: "Another stroke of genius. Because, suddenly, what was once purely male territory is now where you're looking your best." Some people seem to think that women want—or should want—whatever men have. Even their underwear. For some people, that thinking extends to women's behavior as well. Whatever men have or do, the thinking goes, must be the best.

Many women, however, are just about as comfortable—and successful—wearing men's undershorts as they are imitating men in the business world. But luckily neither is necessary.

Young Laura, with MBA in hand and her first big job under way, made a few mistakes starting out because she thought she needed to copy the men around her in order to get along. She practiced answering the telephone with a firm, gruff voice. She had heard the male president of the company answer like that, so she figured it was the "right" way and it would give her the same tough, businesslike sound. Soon her new telephone voice became a habit. Every time Laura's sister called, however, she would say, "Laura, are you all right? Is something wrong? Are you *sure* you're okay?" Instead of sounding businesslike, Laura merely appeared tense and upset. And in a way she was strained. Taking on someone else's style is disconcerting. With her sister's encouragement, Laura went back to her own, more sprightly voice. "It was the first of many changes that made me feel more relaxed,'' she says. ''I was playing this game that said I was in business so I had to be businesslike and I had to be buttoned up. Because that's how you get respect. I thought men would respect me if I talked as they did and behaved like them.'' She found, however, that her gruff voice and manner only made her and others around her uncomfortable. Her own style, which is friendly and humorous, will take her further.

The worst tack a working woman can take is to try to act like a man. Men not only feel uncomfortable around such behavior from women, they resent it. Men aren't necessarily sure what they want from women, but they do know they don't want women acting like men.

Women must, of course, follow the same general rules of business as men to get along. If the company style, for instance, is to confirm everything in memos, then a woman working there had better write memos. Women should be aware, however, that there may be extra rules or a few different ones for them. Over many years the firm may have established well-defined standards for judging men on their dress and behavior, but would they necessarily apply the same rules to women? At one company a former employee reapplied after several years of working elsewhere. The male executive making the decision remembered her and ''didn't like her style.'' A consultant to the company learned that what he meant by that was he remembered the woman used the same language as the men when she last worked there. That language included a lot of swearing, which was tolerated from men, but thought improper for a woman. The woman was not rehired.

Senior vice president for personnel and administration at Gannett Madelyn Jennings says, ''I've seen women who are so much one of the boys that they try to take on the macho. Macho is bad enough for the men to have; I don't think we need it too. It's a bit embarrassing. It's the kind of thing that sets men's teeth on edge. Women who are trying hard to act like men make men uncomfortable.

''That's not how you get respect. You should get respect by being who you are, being good at what you do, being interested in others' lives, not just your own, and by not taking a lot that happens too personally. I wouldn't try to ape some male manager just because you think that's the way to be successful. That isn't going to work.''

Not only is imitating men unwise because it makes men uneasy, but it also denies women the opportunity to create and develop their own professional styles—which just may sometimes be better than men's ways. Men aren't always good managers and don't always do the right things. ''There are a lot of mistakes that have been made in the workplace in terms of treatment of people,'' says Madelyn Jennings. ''We women have something to add to helping people be all they can be.

''We have the chance to be more gentle, more generous—aping men's pride and prejudices is boorish and certainly not going to help us all grow as new leaders in the eighties. Being more gentle, more generous isn't a feminine cop-out, it can be refreshingly human. I once heard Eliza Kellas, the first president of Russell Sage College, described this way: 'A perfect woman, nobly planned, to warn, to comfort, and *command*.' ''*

THE CREDIBILITY GAP

Once a woman learns to operate in her own style, she's made a significant step toward closing the credibility gap, the biggest gender gap of all. Men—and, sadly enough, many women as well—don't assume women have the wherewithal to be successful. Women have to prove themselves again and again in situations where men are assumed to be in charge and competent. A woman president of a large commercial construction company has many times gone to meet new clients (always male) accompanied by one of her male vice presidents. Invariably the male client will come forward to shake hands and introduce himself to the vice president. The woman is either not seen by the men or, if seen, she's disregarded.

*William Wordsworth, ''She Was a Phantom of Delight.''

Sometimes men are blind to the competence of the women they know best. Maggie grew up on a farm, dreaming of taking over the business one day. Her brother showed no interest in farming and left home. Maggie worked the farm alongside her father and then took charge when he grew too old to handle the work. Her father saw her help as temporary and worried mightily about who would take over the business. Even with Maggie doing the work right before his eyes, he couldn't see her contributions and doubted her ability. She eventually confronted him and fought, successfully, to take over. She now has a farm, but she is still stunned by her father's lack of confidence in her. And so it is with many women. Closing that credibility gap is the most difficult task facing women. But every time a woman performs well at work, every time a woman takes on a job performed only by men in the past, every time a woman succeeds in large or small ways, the gap narrows a little.

Proving Competence

Generally women learn two discouraging facts soon after entering the male-dominated business world. The first is that no one will give them the benefit of the doubt. As a result, they'll have to prove their worth again and again.

Most women know that competence is essential, fundamental, to achieving any kind of success. More difficult is facing the fact that they will have to repeatedly demonstrate their competence. Women find that true even at high levels. "Women have to prove they're good, and they have to prove it over and over again. I don't think it ever stops," says a woman executive. "There's an added pressure for women all the time. Can she really do it? Can she really make it? It's very tiring and very demanding and the stress factor is enormous."

Women have to work harder, sacrifice more in their personal lives, and be better than men in order to succeed. That added pressure can discourage and depress even the stalwart. One woman who has worked her way up in a high-tech business over the past ten years, and is still far from where she wants to be, says: "I've always just wanted to do what I'm good at. I've never been anything but an A player —so why do I have to validate myself every day? Sometimes I just want to hang it up—jump in a camper and get out of here."

The second discouraging fact women confront is that they can't be just good; they must be exceptional—often far better than men doing the same job. While men are permitted a certain amount of mediocrity in the working world, few women are.

There are two reasons for this: the credibility gap and simple sexism. Many men find it hard to believe a woman can be good at something men are good at; therefore she has to be *really* good for it to sink in. Says Meredith Fernstrom, "There is usually more demanded of women than there is of men in terms of the quality and quantity of the work. All things being equal, men will be somewhat more tolerant of male workers than they will of women."

In a study of how groups determine leaders, conducted by Diane Keyser Wentworth and Lynn R. Anderson, it was found that displaying expert knowledge of the subject and task at hand was more important for women than men. It was less critical for a man to do that, "since his traditional sex role already includes the notion of leadership." The researchers concluded: "Because women have traditionally been associated with the follower role, not the leader role, it is especially critical that they display expert knowledge about a task in order that other group members will look beyond the female sex role."

The other reason women have to be more competent than men is that competence is not the only factor that determines success in the working world. When an employer is considering a candidate for promotion or hire, work experience and competence is considered, but important also is how well the employer expects that person to fit into the culture of the office or company or group—and that culture is usually a male one. Consultant Denise Cavanaugh uses a point system to explain why women have to be better than men. A man, let's say, might be at 50 points in competence, which is pretty good, but not great. In culture, however, he might have a high 75 points. That means he shares the boss's values and interests; he's one of the guys and the boss can expect to feel comfortable with him. A woman vying for the same position, on the other hand, might have only 30 points in culture simply because she's a woman. Her competence score must be considerably higher than the man's to get the job.

The notion that women must be and are more competent than men is fairly well accepted. A *New York Times* poll found that 80 percent of women and 68 percent of men agree that for a woman to get ahead she must be better at what she does than a man must.

That women have to be better than men seems one of the great injustices of our time. Yet oddly enough, it's not all detrimental. One result is that women who do reach high levels are building the reputation that women are very good at whatever they do. And some men are aware of the extra burden on women. Attorney and businessman Ray Siehndel says, "Men can go out and do the job; a woman has to go out and prove herself as well as do the job. She's probably being critiqued at a higher level than men." That's the reason, he thinks, that so many women he encounters in his work are highly motivated. "They've got a lot of internal drive. They work long hours and are very conscientious."

Madelyn Jennings says she still finds it to be so that women have "to be a little better to be thought of as good." But she's also seeing some payoff to that. A couple of executives in her company have told her that they can look at the track records and see that their female sales representatives have done a better job overall than the men. As a result, they are eager to interview female candidates when openings occur. That's both amusing and gratifying to Jennings who, when she worked at General Electric Company many years ago, was involved in getting the first female sales representative hired in the chemical division of GE. At the time, the GE manager was concerned—perhaps rightly—about whether the account executives of other companies would even see her. "It's a wonderful thing," says Jennings, "for me to compare that, on one hand, to this comment from a couple of executives I know who say, 'Absolutely, I want a woman for that sales job.' "

Despite those encouraging words from the field, many women understandably resent having to continually prove themselves and be judged at a higher level. But the sooner a woman gets over the hump of assuming or wanting fairness in business, the easier work will be for her. Once you know that being good at your job isn't enough, then you can go on to learn the other things you need to know to rise to your level of competence. Says an executive woman: "It's the positioning, it's the merchandising, it's the politics that's important, and it's got to be learned." Don't waste energy resenting that, just *be* better and start learning it.

Being Good Isn't Good Enough

Women who are exceptionally competent, as many are, can come to rely too much on their skills and knowledge and neglect the important area of building relationships with their male colleagues. Competence is vital to success, but so is getting along with people and easing your way into the inner circles—often male-dominated —of whatever company or division or staff or department you're in. Women have particular difficulty doing that sometimes because of the comfort and credibility gaps. Women must be extra diligent, as a result, in paying attention to personal relationships and to the intangibles of the job. They must learn to compete with friends and cooperate with enemies.

Madelyn Jennings offers this advice: "If you are competent—and let's take that as a given—the style, the way a woman handles herself in terms of self-confidence, her sense of humor (which is notably missing in many cases) has a lot to do with being one of the inner circle. Some women threaten through their demeanor, which can be an icy professionalism. Being human, having a sense of humor, not being arrogant about feminism, but rather acting as if you're equal instead of expecting to be treated equally is what is important. It never occurs to me that I'm not equal. When I walk in the door, there's no question in my mind about being equal, but I don't wear it on my sleeve.''

Building relationships with men and making men comfortable, as discussed in Chapter 7, is critical to closing the credibility gap. Grey Advertising's Carolyn Carter says she has found that there is more to the idea that men grow up learning how to work with others—and females don't—than she thought there was. ''The striving for perfection that sometimes typifies women can be very, very helpful,'' says Carolyn. ''It is called being driven and it's part of every successful woman I know. But if you can't build a bridge between yourself and your co-workers and yourself and the people you report to, then being driven and being good isn't enough. That's why we have to work at building those bridges.''

A woman can make serious mistakes if she gets so caught up in doing the job perfectly that she neglects the politics of goodwill. A woman vice president in a young, growing company was reviewing some figures that were to go into the annual report and found an error made by a man who was very powerful and well connected in the company. She went to him with the mistake, and he denied that it was an error. He said it was merely a different interpretation of some numbers. Not content with that explanation and unable to rest with the possibility of a mistake going into the annual report, the woman went over the man's head to senior management. She told them the print order on the annual report should be stopped. And she created a mess. The annual report ended up being printed with the mistake—if it was one—and the woman succeeded only in antagonizing all of senior management.

It may have taken courage for that woman to fight for what she believed was true, but she chose her battle poorly and hurt her chances for further advancement. She was thereafter seen by the senior vice presidents as a troublemaker, and she was the one who earned a reputation as a careless worker. Instead of being so concerned that every detail in the annual report be meticulously correct that she was willing to throw the entire report into disarray, she would have been better off managing her relationships. She could still have let her peer, the man who made the "error," know she disagreed with his interpretation, and she could have written a memo to him or to her file to cover herself. She should then have *let it go*. If there were to be any repercussions over the controversial number, he would have to take the rap, not she. Instead, with a zealot's energy, she tackled a problem and only damaged herself.

High Visibility

Part of maintaining and achieving good relationships with men is making sure they know you're around. For all the reasons discussed so far, women tend to get lost, to be excluded from the important battles that go on between men. To counter that, a woman has to keep reminding men of her presence in a positive way. But that often requires subtle actions rather than the broad strokes one might be tempted to try. Daniela Kuper, owner of an advertising agency, expresses the confusion she felt when she started out in business. It's a confusion many women share, though not all resolve it with the wisdom Kuper did.

"In the beginning you could have put a hat and cane in my hand," she says. "I felt I had to keep everyone's attention and make everyone happy. What a ridiculously tiring thing to do. At some point, I put the hat down and put the cane down and I took a good look at what the other guy was doing and I thought, 'What is he looking for? Let me listen a little harder, how can I communicate? What is he really saying?' I've trained myself to become an observer instead of a performer."

Kuper, like many women, found she had tendencies "that just come with being a woman," which she has learned to control because they don't help her in doing business with men. The tendencies, she says, include "acquiescing or reacting too quickly or reacting emotionally or blurting out your opinion because you believe something." By learning to be an observer instead of a performer, she has improved her ability to work with men. Being an observer isn't easy, however. "It takes a lot of power to shut up," she says. "There's tremendous strength in observing and in responding only when you add to the situation."

The risk for women who take that course is that they'll fade into the woodwork. If you choose an observant approach, then when you do say something it carries more weight and is listened to more carefully. As a result, it had better be worth listening to. Says Kuper: "You'd better measure your thoughts and be intelligent. Otherwise when your turn to speak comes, everyone will think, 'So what?' And you *really* will be in trouble. You'd better get the hat and cane and exit quick!"

As contradictory as this advice may seem, to simultaneously stay visible and be a careful observer, it is not. To be visible in positive ways requires that you be a good observer in order to find out what others are interested in, where their vulnerabilities and strengths are, what they're working on that you could contribute to (or that they could offer to you).

Meredith Fernstrom says that one of her techniques for keeping visible is to be aware of the personal interests of men she works with. If she sees an article in a magazine on the subject, she might then clip it and send it along to him with a note. She also makes a point at American Express social functions to introduce her husband to key members of management. And she never overlooks meeting their wives. "I don't do it in a pushy way," she says, "but in a peer relationship." The nuggets of information she picks up are useful in helping her build the informal networks of information and relationships so important to getting along with others. Meredith also monitors what others in the company do to keep visible. One of the men in the marketing area of her company, for example, found out the birthdays of various people in the company and he calls them every year to wish them happy returns. It's a charming, simple, and effective technique for keeping visible. Now that Meredith has learned his birth date, she makes certain she calls him every year.

THE GULF BETWEEN THE SEXES

A paradox in the work world creates a problem for women. Women must be aware of and must be able to communicate to men the subtle discrimination that keeps women from advancing. The paradox is that women must also forget the discrimination; intense awareness of how difficult a time they have at work distracts and discourages those who dwell on it.

Men cannot understand that simply being a woman can haunt a working woman. A male lawyer in a prominent Washington, D.C., firm is frustrated by the attitudes of some women in his office because he doesn't understand the conflict women face. In his view, the women seem to think that whenever they don't get something they want, it's because they are women. "Look," he said, "at these levels the pyramid is very steep. You go from eighty people on one step to five on the next. I really think women lose sight of that fact."

Most women do know that a lot of men don't make it either. But what men don't know is that when a woman doesn't succeed—in the broad sense or on any one individual project—she can't be certain whether it was due to something she did or didn't do, or because she belongs to the category called *woman*. Men don't have that nagging doubt. If you're a white male and fail, you must, of course, deal with that failure, but without the powerless frustration and anger felt by women who suspect they've been discriminated against. If a man isn't succeeding, he can go about changing his behavior and improving his skills in a more unclouded way. For women, there is often the suspicion that no matter how much she works on her skills, her behavior, she'll never quite fit. She can't alter being a woman. The better the sexes understand one another, the closer we'll come to closing that gap.

Sympathizing with Men

Women who are successful working with men are usually the ones who like men and who try to understand the male point of view.

They also try to communicate the problems and conflicts that face women. The more such communication, the more likely the credibility gap will close. Successful women are also compassionate women who understand the problems and conflicts of both sexes on the job. They understand that work life is often difficult for men, too. "I've seen men turn to alcohol and to drugs," says executive Dorothy Gregg. "I've seen families broken up; I've seen men weep; I've seen men break down completely and have to be taken away. When you have, as I have, been working for twenty-five years in corporations, you even see men kill themselves. It is a great shock and gives you a different perspective on men. I see the tragedy and frustration of men in the corporate world, too, and I have a lot of feeling for it. I think if you can't feel empathy you're lost."

If a woman doesn't at least try to understand men or, worse, if she feels hostility toward men, she'll only widen the credibility gap.

Building Trust

When men learn that they can trust women in business situations, the gulf between the sexes will be considerably narrowed. At all levels of business, but in particular at the higher ranks, workers are judged according to certain traits that go far beyond competence and skill. The most important consideration a boss makes, consciously or unconsciously, when evaluating someone for a promotion, hire, or new assignment, is: Do I trust this person? In tough situations will this person make decisions as I would or use the same decision-making process I would? Will this person handle customers the same as I do? If a man is asking those questions about a woman, the answer to all just might be "no"—or he might have enough doubt in his mind about what the answer should be that he'll say no. A lot of men are eliminated at that stage as well, because the trust judgment is very subtle. The more someone is like ourselves, however, the more likely we are to trust.

Consultant Denise Cavanaugh was working with a department of firefighters who were trying, with some difficulty, to integrate women into the ranks. She found that the biggest concern of the firefighters was whether the others—male or female—could be trusted to go in and pull them out of a fire. Cavanaugh asked them how they could tell whether someone was trustworthy and the men cited such facts as these: "He went to my high school," and, "His mother goes to the same church as my mother." What they were saying was, "He's like me, and I'm a trustworthy person; therefore, he must be trustworthy."

Trust is an issue between workers at all levels, and it may even be the one that is most responsible for keeping women out of the highest positions. Men in top management are under great pressure and are very dependent on other senior managers doing their jobs well. They need each other. If, for instance, the manufacturing plant in Ohio isn't producing at desired levels, the job of the marketing manager in Chicago is going to be all the more difficult. Because of that interdependence, trust is fundamental.

Men often have difficulty trusting women, who are sometimes perceived as being very unlike themselves. Cavanaugh tells about another company she consulted for, where the president was a very hard-driving man who had done well getting women into management in his company. Almost half of his managers were female. One day a crisis occurred and he called in a group of his managers to give him a fast report. In walked three women and he blurted out: "Three women? Where are the boys?" Cavanaugh explains that what he was thinking was "Where are *my* people?" Even that man, who had done a great deal to help women get ahead, had a lapse when he saw women in charge at a moment of crisis.

Men sometimes do learn to trust women and share information with them. Madelyn Jennings believes women can project an image of believability and trust that can pay off. She describes the first staff meeting she attended at one company, when she was grilled by the CEO. "He was testing to see how I would handle being put on the spot with this whole new group of people," she explains. "I didn't handle it particularly well, but I got through it. Later one of the [male] executives took me aside and said, 'Today you were put in the ring, but you won't be at every meeting.' That meant a lot to me.'' Even though she had only been on the job a short time, that executive found her believable enough to extend a useful—and comforting—word to her.

Jennings considers astronaut Sally Ride to be the role model for women today who want to be successful. ''There's no question of her credentials,'' she explains. ''She's smart and competent and well educated. But more important, she's at ease, she's not stuck in status or frills; she's straightforward; *she's someone you feel you can trust*. The test is, if you were backed into a dark corner who would you want on your side? That's a way of defining people. It's not a question of physical strength, but a question of who you can trust and whose brain would be alert and work fast.''

There are a lot of Sally Rides in the work force today. Not all are making headlines, but they are making progress. Every time a woman breaks into a new level, she gives experience with women and how they think to a whole new set of men. A consultant to *Fortune* 500 companies explains it this way: ''Those subtle signals men have learned to read in other men that tell them whether to trust or not have evolved over centuries. Give men a few years with women, and maybe they'll see a whole new set of women's styles and they'll learn to say, 'Hey, I can trust that,' or 'That's a real sign of maturity in a woman,' or 'I can relate that to what I see in men that I trust and respect.' That's where there's hope.''

Part of that hope is dependent on men and women in the workplace accepting women's being a little different. A man needs to learn that the signals from a woman may vary from what he's used to in men and he needs to learn, with help from women, how to judge competence and trust in a woman. Men must learn to develop those instincts with women, just as they have learned them so very well with men. And women must do the same.

The working woman's goal is to retain her warmth and naturalness, to be able to comfort and command, to be respected for being competent, to win in the workplace where men dominate and yet retain her womanliness. To be a CEO or police chief or bank president or senior partner or group supervisor or whatever she wants, and not have to model herself after a man. To be herself and to do her job using all her strengths: That's what a woman wants.

BIBLIOGRAPHY

Abbey, Antonia. "Sex Differences in Attributions for Friendly Behavior: Do Males Misperceive Females' Friendliness?" *Journal of Personality and Social Psychology* 42, no. 5 (1982): 830–838.

Adams, Jane. *Making Good*. New York: Berkley Books, 1983.

Andrews, Lori B. "Exhibit A: Language." *Psychology Today*, Feb. 1984, 28–31.

Asimov, Isaac. "Male Humor." *The New York Times Magazine*, July 17, 1983, 54.

Baruch, Grace, Rosalind Barnett, and Caryl Rivers. *Lifeprints: New Patterns of Love and Work for Today's Woman*. New York: McGraw-Hill, 1983.

Begley, Sharon, and John Carey. "A Healthy Dose of Laughter." *Newsweek*, Oct. 4, 1982, 74.

Berger, Phil. "The New Comediennes." *The New York Times Magazine*, July 29, 1984, 26ff.

Bernikow, Louise. "We're Dancing as Fast as We Can." *Savvy*, Apr. 1984, 40–44.

Bianchi, Suzanne M., and Daphne Spain. *American Women: Three Decades of Change*. U.S. Department of Commerce, Bureau of the Census, 1983.

Callahan-Levy, Charlene M., and Lawrence A. Messe. "Sex Differences in the Allocation of Pay." *Journal of Personality and Social Psychology* 37 (1979): 433–446.

Cantor, Joanne R. "What's Funny to Whom? The Role of Gender." *Journal of Communication* 26 (1976): 164–172.

Chapman, Anthony J., Jean R. Smith, and Hugh C. Foot. "Humour, Laughter, and Social Interaction." In Paul McGhee and Anthony J. Chapman, eds., *Children's Humour*. Chichester, England: John Wiley & Sons, 1980, 141–179.

Chesler, Phyllis, and E. J. Goodman. *Women, Money and Power*. New York: William Morrow, 1976.

Collins, Eliza G. C. "Managers and Lovers." *Harvard Business Review*, Sept.–Oct. 1983, 142–153.

Collins, Eliza G. C., and Timothy B. Blodgett. "Some See It . . . Some Won't." *Harvard Business Review*, Mar.–Apr. 1981, 77–94.

Collins, Glenn. "New Studies on 'Girl Toys' and "Boy Toys.' " *The New York Times*, Feb. 13, 1984, A18.

Coser, Rose Laub. "Some Social Functions of Laughter: A Study of Humor in a Hospital Setting." *Human Relations* 12 (1959): 171–181.

———. "Laughter Among Colleagues: A Study of the Social Functions of Humor Among the Staff of a Mental Hospital." *Psychiatry* 23 (1960): 81–95.

Crosby, Faye. "Selective Vision." *Working Woman*, July 1984, 67–69.

Deaux, Kay. "Sex Differences." In T. Blass, ed., *Personality Variables in Social Behavior*. Hillsdale, N.J.: Ettbaum, 1977, 357–377.

———. "Self-Evaluations of Male and Female Managers." *Sex Roles* 5, no. 5 (1979): 571–580.

Dowd, Maureen. "Many Women in Poll Equate Values of Job and Family Life." *The New York Times*, Dec. 4, 1983, A1ff.

Dullea, Georgia. "The Sexes: Differences in Speech." *The New York Times*, Mar. 19, 1984, C10.

Durden-Smith, Jo, and Diane deSimone. *Sex and the Brain*. New York: Arbor House, 1983.

Ehrenreich, Barbara. "The Politics of Talking in Couples: Conversus Interruptus and Other Disorders." *Ms.*, May 1981, 46ff.

Ellyson, Steve L., John F. Dovidio, and B. J. Fehr. "Visual Behavior and Dominance in Women and Men." In Clara Mayo and Nancy M. Henley, eds., *Gender and Nonverbal Behavior*. New York: Springer-Verlag, 1981, 63–80.

Epstein, Sue Hoover. "Why Do Women Live Longer Than Men?" *Science* 83 (Oct. 1983): 30–31.

Fast, Julius. *Body Language*. New York: Pocket Books, Simon & Schuster, 1970.

Forisha, Barbara, and Barbara H. Goldman. *Outsiders on the Inside: Women and Organizations*. Englewood Cliffs, N.J.: Prentice-Hall, 1981.

Fortune, Apr. 16, 1984, cover.

Freud, Sigmund. *Jokes and Their Relation to the Unconscious*. James Strachey, trans. & ed. New York: W. W. Norton, 1960.

———. "Some Psychical Consequences of the Anatomical Distinction Between the Sexes." In Patrick C. Lee and Robert Sussman Stewart, eds., *Sex Differences: Cultural and Developmental Dimensions*. New York: Urizen Books, 1976, 45–56.

Frieze, Irene. "Being Feminine or Masculine—Nonverbally." In I. H. Frieze, J. Z. Parsons, P. B. Johnson, N. Ruble, and G. L. Zellman, eds.,

Women and Sex Roles: A Social Psychological Perspective. New York: W. W. Norton, 1978, 321–334.

Frieze, Irene Hanson, and Sheila J. Ramsey. "Nonverbal Maintenance of Traditional Sex Roles." *Journal of Social Issues* 32, no. 3 (1976): 133–141.

Gilligan, Carol. *In a Different Voice: Psychological Theory and Women.* Cambridge, Mass.: Harvard University Press, 1982.

Goleman, Daniel. "Psychology Is Revising Its View of Women." *The New York Times*, Mar. 20, 1984, C1–2.

"Good News: We'll Live Longer." *U.S. News & World Report*, May 14, 1984, 13.

Gottfried, Allen W., and Kay Bathurst. "Hand Preference Across Time Is Related to Intelligence in Young Girls, Not Boys." *Science* 221 (Sept. 1983): 1074–1076.

Gould, Robert E., M.D. "Measuring Masculinity by the Size of a Paycheck." In Joseph H. Pleck and Jack Sawyer, eds., *Men and Masculinity*. Englewood Cliffs, N.J.: Prentice-Hall, 1974, 96–100.

Graham, Katharine. "Women and Power." *Folio*, July 1984, 128.

Gross, Amy. "Thinking Like a Woman." *Vogue*, May 1982, 268ff.

Hacker, Andrew. "Women vs. Men in the Work Force." *The New York Times Magazine*, Dec. 9, 1984, 124ff.

Henley, Nancy M. *Body Politics: Power, Sex, and Nonverbal Communication.* Englewood Cliffs, N.J.: Prentice-Hall, 1977.

Hershey, Robert D., Jr. "Women's Pay Fight Shifts to 'Comparable Worth.' " *The New York Times*, Nov. 1, 1983, A15.

"His and Her Brains." *Science* 82 (Sept. 1982): 14.

Horney, Karen, M.D. "The Flight from Womanhood: The Masculinity Complex in Women as Viewed by Men and Women." In Harold Kelman, M.D., ed., *Feminine Psychology*. New York: W. W. Norton, 1967, 54–70.

———. "The Dread of Women: Observations on a Specific Difference in the Dread Felt by Men and Women Respectively for the Opposite Sex." In Harold Kelman, M.D., ed., *Feminine Psychology*. New York: W. W. Norton, 1967, 133–146.

"How Executives See Women in Management." *Business Week*, June 28, 1982, 10.

Johnson, Sharon. "Male-Female Longevity Gap Widening, Doctors Are Told." *The New York Times*, May 22, 1984, C10.

Kanter, Rosabeth Moss. *Men and Women of the Corporation.* New York: Basic Books, 1977.

———. "Power Failure in Management Circuits." *Harvard Business Review*, July–Aug. 1979, 65–75.

————. "Casebook: Influence Skills." *Working Woman*, Sept. 1983, 50ff.

Kennedy, Marilyn Moats. "Job Strategies." *Glamour*, Feb. 1984, 172.

Klemesrud, Judy. "Kentucky's Woman at the Helm." *The New York Times*, May 20, 1984, 62.

Kohlberg, Lawrence. "Moral Stages and Moralization: The Cognitive-Developmental Approach." In Thomas Lickona, ed., *Moral Development and Behavior: Theory, Research, and Social Issues*. New York: Holt, Rinehart and Winston, 1976, 31–53.

Konner, Melvin. *The Tangled Wing: Biological Constraints on the Human Spirit*. New York: Harper & Row, 1983.

————. "Hemispheres Apart." *Science* 83 (Nov. 1983): 96–97.

Korda, Michael. *Power! How to Get It, How to Use It*. New York: Ballantine Books, 1975.

Lacoste-Utamsing, Christine de, and Ralph Holloway. "Sexual Dimorphism in the Human Corpus Callosum." *Science* 216 (June 1982): 1431–1432.

Lakoff, Robin. *Language and Woman's Place*. New York: Harper Colophon Books, Harper & Row, 1975.

Lee, Patrick C. "Introduction." In Patrick C. Lee and Robert Sussman Stewart, eds., *Sex Differences: Cultural and Developmental Dimensions*. New York: Urizen Books, 1976, 13–32.

Leventhal, Gerald S., and David Anderson. "Self-Interest and the Maintenance of Equity." *Journal of Personality and Social Psychology* 15, no. 1 (1970): 57–62.

Leventhal, Gerald S., and Douglas W. Lane. "Sex, Age, and Equity Behavior." *Journal of Personality and Social Psychology* 15, no. 4 (1970): 312–316.

Levinson, Daniel J. *The Seasons of a Man's Life*. New York: Ballantine Books, 1978.

Lorenz, Konrad. *On Aggression*. Marjorie Kerr Wilson, trans. New York: Bantam, 1963.

Maccoby, Eleanor Emmons, and Carol Nagy Jacklin. *The Psychology of Sex Differences*. Stanford, Calif.: Stanford University Press, 1974.

Major, Brenda. "Gender Patterns in Touching Behavior." In Clara Mayo and Nancy M. Henley, eds., *Gender and Nonverbal Behavior*. New York: Springer-Verlag, 1981, 15–38.

Major, Brenda, and Jeffrey B. Adams. "Role of Gender, Interpersonal Orientation, and Self-Presentation in Distributive-Justice Behavior." *Journal of Personality and Social Psychology* 45, no. 3 (1983): 598–608.

McGhee, Paul E. *Humor: Its Origin and Development*. San Francisco: W. H. Freeman, 1979.

Miller, Jean Baker. *Toward a New Psychology of Women*. Boston: Beacon Press, 1976.

Monagan, David. "The Failure of Coed Sports." *Psychology Today*, Mar. 1983, 58ff.

Naftolin, Frederick. "Understanding the Bases of Sex Differences." *Science* 221 (Mar. 1981): 1263–1264.

Naifeh, Steven, and Gregory White Smith. *Why Can't Men Open Up? Overcoming Men's Fear of Intimacy*. New York: Clarkson N. Potter, 1984.

Neely, James C., M.D. *Gender—The Myth of Equality*. New York: Simon & Schuster, 1981.

Norman, Michael. "Standing His Ground." *The New York Times Magazine*, Apr. 1, 1984, 55.

O'Connell, Walter. "An Item Analysis of the Wit and Humor Appreciation Test." *The Journal of Social Psychology* 56 (1962): 271–276.

Parlee, Mary Brown. "Conversational Politics." *Psychology Today*, May 1979, 48–56.

Pear, Robert. "Wage Lag Is Found for White Women." *The New York Times*, Jan. 16, 1984, A1ff.

Person, Ethel Spector, M.D. "Women Working: Fears of Failure, Deviance, and Success." *Journal of the American Academy of Psychoanalysis* 10, no. 1 (1982): 67–84.

Porter, Natalie, and Florence Geis. "Women and Nonverbal Leadership Cues: When Seeing Is Not Believing." In Clara Mayo and Nancy M. Henley, eds., *Gender and Nonverbal Behavior*. New York: Springer-Verlag, 1981, 39–62.

"Profile of Women Senior Executives." Study by Korn/Ferry International, 1982.

Roberts, Steven V. "Women Gain in Power Structure." *The New York Times*, Aug. 13, 1984, A12.

Rubenstein, Carin. "Who Wants to Live 500 Years? Men Do." *Psychology Today*, Mar. 1983, 81.

Safer, Martin. "Sex and Hemisphere Differences in Access to Codes for Processing Emotional Expressions and Faces." *Journal of Experimental Psychology* 110, no. 1 (1981): 86–99.

Scheflen, Albert E. "Quasi-Courtship Behavior in Psychotherapy." *Psychiatry* 28 (1965): 245–257.

Smith, Edward E., and Jacqueline D. Goodchilds. "Characteristics of the Witty Group Member: The Wit as Leader." *American Psychologist* 14 (1959): 375–376.

Sperry, Roger. "Some Effects of Disconnecting the Cerebral Hemisphere." *Science* 217 (Sept. 1982): 1223–1226.

Stein, Sara Bonnett. *Girls & Boys: The Limits of Nonsexist Childrearing.* New York: Charles Scribner's Sons, 1983.

Suplee, Curt. "Why Do We Weep? As Yet, Nobody Can Say for Sure." *Smithsonian*, June 1984, 102ff.

Stockard, Jean, and Miriam M. Johnson. "The Social Origins of Male Dominance." *Sex Roles* 5, no. 2 (1979): 199–218.

Tannen, Deborah. "Conversational Style: When Women & Men Talk— Why Don't We Say What We Mean?" *Vogue*, Oct. 1982, 185ff.

Theroux, Paul. "The Male Myth." *The New York Times Magazine*, Nov. 27, 1983, 116.

Tiger, Lionel. *Men in Groups.* New York: Random House, 1969.

Ullian, Joseph Alan. "Joking at Work." *Journal of Communication* 26 (1976): 129–133.

U.S. Bureau of the Census, *Statistical Abstract of the United States: 1984* (104th edition). Washington, D.C., 1983.

Vaillant, George E. *Adaptation to Life: How the Best and the Brightest Came of Age.* Boston: Little, Brown, 1977.

Wentworth, Diane Keyser, and Lynn R. Anderson. "Emergent Leadership as a Function of Sex and Task Type." *Sex Roles* 11, nos. 5 & 6 (1984): 513–524.

West, Candace, and Donald H. Zimmerman. "Women's Place in Everyday Talk: Reflections on Parent-Child Interaction." *Social Problems* 24, no. 5 (1977): 521–529.

"Why Men Don't Speak Their Minds." *Science Digest*, Nov. 1983, 88.

"Will Women Decide Outcome of the 1984 Elections?" *U.S. News & World Report*, Dec. 12, 1983, 58–60.

"Women Expand Their Roles in Crime, Too." *U.S. News & World Report*, Nov. 12, 1984, 62.

Zeitz, Baila. "The Crisis in Middle Management." *Working Woman*, Sept. 1983, 133ff.

Zillmann, Dolf, and S. Holly Stocking. "Putdown Humor." *Journal of Communication* 26 (1976): 154–163.

INDEX

Books of further interest . . .

THE WORKING WOMAN'S GUIDE

Women have always worked, but it is only in the past century that the idea of a woman with a career has become an accepted — or even possible — concept. Today's working woman is rarely just filling a gap between school and marriage, but many women are still finding themselves judged in this light when it comes to matters like pay, promotion, training, and even job opportunities themselves.

In the age of equal opportunities, Liz Hodgkinson examines the ways in which long-held attitudes, by women as well as men, mean that women are still 'second class' workers, and that a woman at the top of the tree is still something of a rarity. Here, too, is all the advice you need to make the most of every opportunity whether in career planning, interviews for jobs and promotion, combining family with career or going it alone.

A wealth of sound guidance is backed up with listings of further reading and organizations in every field to help you deal best with your own situation, and is enriched with lively and fascinating comments from women who have experienced the struggles and successes which being a working woman brings.

THE SINGLE WOMAN'S SURVIVAL GUIDE

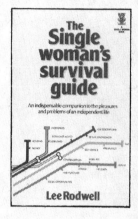

The Single woman's survival guide

An indispensable companion to the pleasures and problems of an independent life

Lee Rodwell

To be single is no longer to be the odd one out. Amongst the swelling ranks of independent women are students, managing on a grant; young working women, sharing flats and planning their futures; career women, paying off a mortgage, perhaps raising children on their own; and all the other permutations and possibilities offered by the changes and opportunities which the past decades have brought about.

But with these changes have come situations unique to the new status of the single woman, and old attitudes to 'spinsterhood' are, in some cases, taking a long time to die.

Lee Rodwell has compiled a wide range of essential information — spiced with fascinating background research and reading, and invaluable personal accounts — which will help the single woman not merely survive but actually enjoy and benefit most from the freedom which independence brings.